D1179818

Old Greenwood
Pathfinder of the West

OLD GREENWOOD · PATHFINDER OF THE WEST
BY ALEXANDER L. CROSBY

Based upon the book by
CHARLES KELLY AND DALE L. MORGAN

Maps by Fred Kliem

THE TALISMAN PRESS
Georgetown, California 1967

TO NANCY
who taught an old dog
a new trade

ACKNOWLEDGMENT

Most of the material in this book was taken from the scholarly volume by Charles Kelly and Dale L. Morgan, *Old Greenwood—The Story of Caleb Greenwood: Trapper, Pathfinder and Early Pioneer.* Published in 1965 by The Talisman Press, this was a revised edition of Charles Kelly's 1936 work. It is now out of print.

To round out the chapters about the fur trade, the tragedy of the Donner party and some other sections, two other books were used extensively. They are *Overland in 1846: Diaries and Letters of the California-Oregon Trail* by Dale Morgan (The Talisman Press, 1963), and *The American Fur Trade of the Far West* by Hiram Martin Chittenden (Academic Reprints, Stanford, 1954).

My warmest thanks go to Charles Kelly, for reading the manuscript and improving the last chapter; to Robert Greenwood and Newton Baird of The Talisman Press, for ideal working conditions; to Helen Papashvily, for finding old pictures instantly; to Margaret Walp, for beautiful typing; and, most particularly, to my wife, Nancy Larrick, who read the manuscript three times and suggested scores of changes, nearly all of which were made.

ALEXANDER L. CROSBY

Quakertown, Pennsylvania
25 October 1967

CONTENTS

How tools and water were used to find California's gold in 1849.

I

Gold Lake

O N   A   SPRING   DAY   IN   1849 a half-dozen miners were sitting around a log cabin in Coloma, California. The
topic was the one that never bored anyone: gold. The cabin
belonged to Caleb Greenwood, an 86-year-old pioneer and
pathfinder of the west. It stood not far from the spot where
James W. Marshall had discovered gold a year before.

Old Greenwood's rough cabin was a social center. After
panning for gold in one of the forks of the American River
or searching the hills for signs of the precious stuff, the
miners would gather at Greenwood's place to hear his end-
less tales of adventures. The old mountain man had trapped
and hunted all over the west. He had led the first wagon
train across the Sierra Nevada. He had fought the Indians
—yet he had married an Indian woman, the mother of his
daredevil sons. He had had many narrow escapes from
death, although probably not so many as he told about. He
was known throughout the mining camp as a dead shot and
he was never far from his rifle.

Caleb was not much interested in seeking gold for himself. The life of a miner was hard work, day after day, often
for only a few dollars or nothing at all. But the old mountain man understood the fever that had drawn thousands
of men to California from all over the United States and
Europe. And on this particular spring day he had a story
that stunned his listeners into silence.

9

Some years ago, Caleb said, he had camped in the mountains by a sparkling lake. The shores of the lake were covered with gold nuggets. All a man had to do was pick them up. Since Caleb had no use for gold then, and no way to sell it, he had left behind what may have been the greatest fortune in the world.

Old Greenwood bit off a chew of tobacco as the excited miners shot questions at him. "Where was the lake?" "How big were the nuggets?" "Are you sure they were gold?" "Could you find the lake again?"

The old man chewed for a few moments. Sure, it was gold. Yes, he knew where the lake was. It was off to the northeast, high in the Sierra Nevada. He didn't want to go there again, but if the group would handsomely outfit his son John, he would send him as a pilot. Of course, he would need to have something for himself, in advance.

One of the miners who heard Old Greenwood tell about Gold Lake that day was Henry DeGroot, who had come from New York to find a fortune. DeGroot had made friends with a party of young Oregonians who gave him permission to join them on a rich bar of the Middle Fork of the American River, about 16 miles from Coloma. Five of the Oregonians were killed by Indians and their claim became known as Murderer's Bar. DeGroot escaped the massacre because he was trying to find his horses.

Twenty-five years later DeGroot wrote the story of Gold Lake and explained why the miners believed Caleb:

Now, Greenwood had a bad reputation for truth and sobriety. Indeed, his powers of falsification were quite phenomenal; to say that he was an habitual liar would mislead, as leaving room for the inference that he sometimes spoke the truth. Yet in this particular instance, while his statements might be exaggerated, there must, we thought, be some foundation for them, or he would hardly suffer his son to go off on such an errand.

10

So the miners provided Caleb with a liberal supply of whisky and a few other necessities, rigged out John in first-class style, and sent him at the head of a company of 13 to find Gold Lake and report on its exact location. Provisions were carried on several pack animals, which would bring back the first shipment of gold.

DeGroot paid his share of the expedition's costs, but could not go himself because he had started two sidelines: packing supplies and trading. (The gold-seekers paid dearly for freight. A typical charge was $20 for hauling 100 pounds from Sutter's to Coloma, a distance of roughly 40 miles.) The rules of the company permitted DeGroot to send a substitute. He chose a Norwegian sailor who had run away from his ship, as many hundreds of other seamen had done, and arrived at the sawmill a day or two earlier. The seaman was glad to get deeper into the mountains, in case he was being pursued.

Days passed. DeGroot, like those in the expedition, often indulged in one of the most delightful occupations of human beings: imagining what he would do if he had a fortune.

After almost a month had elapsed, the party returned, ragged, hungry and totally disgusted. They had found several lakes, but not a speck of gold could be seen at any of them. Old Greenwood was asked for an explanation. He replied calmly that John had missed the right lake with the genuine gold. The "stuff" he had seen "war that, shure."

DeGroot was not satisfied with this explanation. Some time later, when Old Greenwood had moved over the hills to Greenwood Valley (lying between the South and Middle Forks of the American River), the young miner stopped at his camp. He spoke plainly to Caleb about sending the expedition on a vain search for gold. Caleb listened in silence. DeGroot became bolder, finally calling the old mountain man a cheat and a liar.

At this point Old Greenwood rose from the log where

11

he had been sitting. He answered DeGroot in this fashion:

"Look a-har, young man; I reckon thar ain't no use for this onpleasantness atween gentlemen. See them yar?" He pointed to several rifles stacked against a tree at the door of his tent. "All fixed for service, and shure to carry lead whar ye pint 'em; take yer choice, stranger, and measure off yer groun'—I'm not perticular 'bout distance."

A duel with Greenwood was the last thing that DeGroot wanted. Although the old man's eyes were as "red as those of a pigeon through a long continued use of liquor," the mountaineer was never known to miss. DeGroot tried to escape from his jam by saying it wouldn't look well for a young man to fight a person of his years, with eyesight impaired by age.

Old Greenwood quickly put a stop to this talk. Pointing to his eyes, the old man said:

"Y'ain't nothin' ails them yar eyes, stranger—yain't no varmint lives onto wich they ever drawed bead! Jes' step off nigh onto yon bush," he continued, tossing a chip toward a manzanita a little way off, "step off about thar, an' I reckon we can settle this yar difficulty like white men orter."

DeGroot had two choices: unconditional surrender, or certain death. He quickly decided he would rather live, so, without any more quibbling, he backed down. Then, knowing it was good policy for packers and other animal owners to be on good terms with the Greenwood family, he went to his pack train and got a plug of tobacco. Pretending to bite off a chew for himself, he handed the plug to Caleb. The old man took a mouthful and dropped the plug into the pocket of his hunting shirt. The quarrel was ended.

To guarantee peace in the future, DeGroot brought a small keg to Caleb on his next trip. The contents extinguished the last spark of resentment smouldering in the old man's breast. From time to time DeGroot made similar gifts, and few visitors to Greenwood's camp were more

12

Sutter's Fort as it looked many years ago, before restoration.

welcome than the brash New Yorker who had dared to speak his mind about Gold Lake.

The legend of Gold Lake did not die. A quite different version was published in 1880 in the *History of Nevada County, California,* taken from an article in the *Nevada Daily Gazette.* In this account, Old Greenwood had come to Sutter's to see the new town of Sacramento that was springing up around the fort. He dropped in at a gambling saloon where several men were examining some nuggets spread on a table. Greenwood was much interested to hear that these yellow chunks were gold, which he pretended not to recognize. Then, with a small audience listening closely, he began to spin his tale. A few years ago he had spent several weeks with his family in a little valley high up in the Sierra. While he hunted, his children played around the camp. They collected a lot of these smooth yellow stones for playthings, and when they left they took a few

13

Greenwood, California, about 1863. See page 135 for 1967 view.

of the smallest with them. But even these became too heavy, and since the children were tired of them, he threw them away.

Caleb's matter-of-fact tone and venerable face convinced his listeners that he was telling the truth. They promptly invited him to a private room, where they put a bottle of whisky before him and pressed him for directions to the little valley with the yellow rocks. He was quite willing to talk. The route was to the head of Bear River, then across several ridges to the little valley, which was near the summit of the Sierra. To make the search easier, he drew a rough map on the table.

Finally, in a mellow frame of mind, Caleb suggested that his new friends come to his camp in Greenwood Valley. He would pilot them to the valley of their dreams.

The excited miners reached Caleb's tent a few days later, well equipped for the expedition. But the old man was on the point of death and soon expired. After his burial the visitors talked to his son. Did he remember the valley with the yellow pebbles? The boy did. He was sure he would recognize it if he saw it; perhaps he could guide them to it.

14

So the party set forth, following the Bear River to Bear Valley, then crossing a ridge to Two-Mile Valley. At this point the directions given by Caleb did not fit the landscape. The landmarks he had described could not be found, and his son's memory was of no help. The miners wandered through hills and valleys until their food and their hopes gave out, then returned in sadness.

Comparing this story with DeGroot's account of Gold Lake, Charles Kelly and Dale Morgan concluded that the newspaper story was a piece of fiction. Caleb was not the first to create a golden fairy tale, and others may have tried to improve on the old master's handiwork.

"But surely Old Greenwood, who loved a good story and concocted his share, would have enjoyed knowing that his Gold Lake fable would come down through the ages, part of the ineradicable romance of the Gold Rush," Kelly and Morgan wrote.

In 1850, a year after Caleb's invention of Gold Lake, the fable was still taken seriously. A miner who had heard the story passed it on, and within a few weeks hundreds of miners were tramping the mountains in search of the mythical lake.

Alexander L. Crosby

An old mine car is a relic of Greenwood's past.

15

2
Young Greenwood

ALTHOUGH CALEB GREENWOOD WAS ONE of the great explorers of the West, his life is a picture puzzle with most of the pieces missing. Old Greenwood, as he was known from the Missouri River to San Francisco, kept no diary and wrote no letters. He did not know how to write. But few men could equal him in aiming a gun, finding a trail and feeding on game and fish. He could live like an Indian, and for much of his life he did.

Most of the men who blazed trails through the unknown Indian country were very young. Kit Carson was only 16 when he ran away to Santa Fe and became a trapper and scout. The famous mountain man, Jim Bridger, was 18 when he quit a blacksmith's job in St. Louis to join William H. Ashley's fur-trading expedition up the Missouri River in 1822. And the United States government entrusted 29-year-old Lieutenant Joseph C. Ives with the task of exploring the Colorado River by steamboat in 1857.

Caleb Greenwood headed toward the frontier as a youth but he did not achieve fame until his sixties. And this giant of a man was 84 when he went to the rescue of the starving Donner party, trapped by the deep snows of the Sierra Nevada, in 1847.

The early years of Greenwood are almost unknown. He was probably born in Virginia in 1763. There is a story, told many years ago by the widow of his son William, that Caleb had to flee from home at the age of 18. His father had put up security for a neighbor who had borrowed money. The man couldn't pay. The lender had taken a fancy to the Greenwoods' Negro cook, and he decided to take her instead of the money. Before daylight one morning he came with the sheriff. The two men seized the woman when she went outdoors to gather kindling. Hearing her screams, Caleb ran out with his rifle as the cook was being dragged away. He fired; one man fell, the other ran off. Caleb went back to the house and said he had just shot a man. The boy's father took a lantern and discovered the lifeless body of the sheriff. Fearing that Caleb might be sent to prison, the father told him to leave Virginia.

Where he went no one knows, but it seems likely that he traveled across the mountains to Tennessee or Kentucky. Later he moved farther west to the Indian territory. In 1834 Caleb told a missionary he had been living in the Indian country for 26 years, or ever since 1808.

Hundreds of mountain men were roaming through the Indian country in the early 1800s, seeking an animal with valuable brown fur. The animal was the beaver. A single skin was worth $4 to $12, and that was a lot of money in those times. The price was high because beaver fur was used in making men's hats, which were therefore called "beavers."

As the trappers wiped out colony after colony of beavers, they kept pushing west in search of more colonies along the streams and rivers of the Rocky Mountains.

In New York, a German immigrant named John Jacob Astor became excited over Lewis and Clark's great expedition to the Pacific Coast in 1806. Astor, already rich and determined to be richer, saw a chance to build up his fur business by tapping new lands of the far west. He set up two expeditions, one to travel by sea around Cape Horn, the other to move up the Missouri River from St. Louis and then cross the Rockies.

17

A buckskin-clad trapper of the early 19th century, seeking beaver.

The overland party left St. Louis in October 1810, its three boats well loaded with hunters, trappers, boatmen and supplies. After traveling more than 400 miles, the party established a winter camp at the mouth of the Nodaway River, north of the present city of St. Joseph, Missouri. Wild turkeys and deer were plentiful. There would be no shortage of food while the river was frozen.

Here, at the winter camp where the Nodaway joins the Missouri, we find the first written record of Caleb Greenwood. His name appears several times in the account book of the expedition. John Jacob Astor wanted records kept of all transactions, and he saved the account books. Today those handwritten accounts of 1810 and 1811 are in the Baker Library at Harvard University.

... *Leonard Lee Rue III*

The ancestors of this beaver escaped the man on the opposite page.

Apparently Caleb joined the expedition as a hunter at the winter camp, for his name is not listed earlier. He bought $32 worth of supplies from December 3, 1810, to January 27, 1811. He got a powder horn for $1.50, a rifle lock for $6, three blankets for $4, a knife for 75 cents, a pack of cards for $2, two shirts at $2 each, cotton handkerchiefs, tobacco and other items. Then, mysteriously, he left the expedition before it made its famous crossing of the continent to the Columbia River.

Did Greenwood have a falling-out with the leaders? Did he doubt their ability to reach the Columbia? Or did he simply decide to stay in the Missouri country? We do not know. But we do know that a year later he showed up in Fort Osage, Missouri, working for a rival of Astor.

19

3
Trapper on the Missouri

ALTHOUGH JOHN JACOB ASTOR WAS A RICH and powerful merchant in 1812, he had not yet built a monopoly
in the fur trade. One of his rivals was Manuel Lisa of the
Missouri Fur Company. Lisa was a tough Spaniard who
braved hostile Indians in his quest for skins.

In May 1812, Lisa started up the Missouri River from
St. Louis with two boats, manned chiefly with Frenchmen
from Canada. But there were some United States citizens
aboard and also a German, John C. Luttig, who kept a
journal for almost a year. On June 4, Luttig noted that
at Fort Osage two hunters had joined the party. One of
them was Greenwood.

By then Caleb was 49 years old and still unmarried. He
may have wanted a change from the lonely life of a hunter.
He may have needed money. Whatever his reasons, he had
chosen an expedition that promised hard work, excitement
and danger. Although Luttig's diary seldom mentions
Caleb by name, we can get a vivid picture of his life from
the notes that were kept by the German immigrant.

Two days after the hunters had come aboard, they killed
three bears, three deer and one turkey. Meat was roasted
in a camp opposite the Kansas River after a day's journey
of 15 miles.

The voyage up the Missouri was one hardship after another. The boats were slowed or stopped by sandbars, float-

ing tree trunks and half-buried stumps. Sometimes the oarsmen could make no headway against the current, even with the help of poles and a sail. Then the boat would be cordelled. Men would jump into the water, carrying a line (or cordel) and tow the craft upstream. If there was no foothold along the banks, a rope would be tied to a tree ahead. The other end would be wound on a windlass, pulling the boat forward foot by foot.

A day's log of more than 30 miles was unusual. The men were generally satisfied with 20 miles, and often they traveled much less. On one miserable day, while Lisa's boat was being cordelled, the current tore it loose from the men on the bank. The few men left on board finally landed it far downstream, where they had spent the night before. More than once the rudder was broken by hidden rocks or tree trunks, and high winds could snap the mast. Replacements had to be made from green lumber ashore.

On the Fourth of July, the voyagers were awakened at 2 a.m. by what Luttig called "a salute from heaven"—a terrific thunderstorm. The heavy rain caved in the river bank, and Lisa was almost drowned. The men jumped into their boats for safety, rowing and poling all day against a stiff current. Finally they were relieved by a favorable wind.

Nearly every day Greenwood and his fellow hunters brought in game. Deer were most plentiful, but the expedition fed also on duck, goose, turkey, fish, rabbit, elk, bear and buffalo. Sunday, August 16, was a big day. The hunters killed 11 buffalo and 11 ducks and caught 11 catfish.

The Missouri claimed more than one life as the two boats worked their way past sandbars and through twisting channels. One of the Frenchmen fell overboard as he was poling and disappeared, probably trapped under the roots of a tree. A Negro boy owned by Lisa went ashore to gather grass for a pet prairie dog. He fell from a cliff into the river and was swept away.

21

The upper Missouri, as it looked during Caleb Greenwood's voyage.

One tragedy was prevented. After the usual daylight start one morning, the expedition stopped for breakfast when the sun was well up. Luttig noticed that the company's pet cat was missing. Lisa sent a man back to the overnight camp site to search for her, and at twilight the cat-hunter overtook the party, puss in arms. He was welcomed with a rousing cheer after his 12-mile hike.

"An Animal of this kind is more valuable in this Country than a fine Horse," Luttig wrote. "Mice are in great abundance and the Company have lost for want of Cats, several Thousand Dollars in Merchandize.... there has not a night passed since our departure from Bellefontaine where I got that Cat, that she has not caught from 4 to 10 Mice and brought them to her Kittens."

The mouse population on Luttig's boat must have been enormous. If the cat averaged seven mice a night, there would have been 580 deaths since the party left Bellefontaine. Apparently there was a pretty fair number of births, too.

The Indians did not look kindly on the whites who were entering their territory in larger and larger numbers. Lisa and other fur traders kept peace by making presents to the chiefs and by being ready to use their guns. The Arikaras gave permission to Lisa that summer to build a fort 12 miles above their village so furs and supplies could be stored during the winter. This was Fort Manuel, just south of the present boundary between North and South Dakota.

At that time the tribesmen of the Missouri country were busier making war on each other than in attacking the whites. The Arikaras were being hounded by raiders from the Gros Ventre tribe, commonly called the Bigbellies. Two white hunters had also been killed by the Bigbellies, and the Indians had taken more than 20 horses. Lisa set out with an armed band of 26 men, no doubt including Greenwood, to demand return of the horses. The resourceful Spaniard got the animals, but he had to trade merchandise for them.

On the day that Lisa returned, the account book shows that Greenwood was charged $4 for a pack of cards. Caleb probably felt he had earned some relaxation after facing the Bigbellies.

Lisa's Fort Manuel was built on a bluff overlooking the river. The prairie, where thousands of buffalo roamed, stretched out to the hazy horizon. In the river bottom, there was an abundance of timber which was felled and trimmed to make a provision house and a blacksmith shop. The men worked hard, for even in August the weather was turning cold.

Trading with the Indians for their furs began on August 28, and two days later a boat laden with the precious cargo began the four-week journey down the river to St. Louis.

23

That day Caleb Greenwood was charged for four twists of tobacco.

Prices were high at Fort Manuel. True, it was hard to haul merchandise up the stubborn Missouri, but Manuel Lisa could charge what he liked because there was no other store within hundreds of miles. Thus Caleb had to pay $2 for a file and $6 for a shirt. He also bought cloth, thread and vermilion, the bright red pigment. All of these were cherished by Indian women, and it was prudent and pleasant for a man to bring proper gifts to the natives.

Early in September, Greenwood became a trapper rather than a hunter, although he would never give up hunting. Together with six other trappers under a Missouri Fur Company man, Caleb set out for the Crow country and the Little Big Horn River. He came back to Fort Manuel in January, bringing 31 beaver skins for which he was credited at $4 each. Then he went back into the Crow country with the other trappers.

The men returned to the fort at the end of March with more skins, but there is no record of Caleb bringing any. So, when the Missouri Fur Company settled up with the trappers on April 30, 1812, Caleb actually owed $211 for his dangerous year along the Missouri and in the Crow country. He signed a note for this amount and probably returned to St. Louis with Lisa. The War of 1812 was underway, and the British were encouraging the Indians to attack the trappers. The life of a mountain man had become almost as risky as that of a beaver.

4
A Perilous Journey

IN 1764, A TALENTED 14-year-old boy named René Auguste Chouteau sailed up the Mississippi River from New Orleans. He was in charge of some 30 mechanics, whom he put to work felling trees and building cabins on a bluff. The site had been selected a few months earlier by his older friend, Pierre Laclede Liguest, partner in a trading company. The settlement, named St. Louis, was then in French territory.

Forty years later St. Louis became part of the United States. By 1810, the population was 1,400, and the town was thriving from the fur trade. Down the Missouri came canoes and the first keelboats loaded with precious skins. Bundles of pelts also arrived by packhorse and even on a few human backs. After disposing of their furs, the trappers and traders bought supplies for their next venture into the wilderness.

Caleb Greenwood probably spent the two years of 1813-1815 in the vicinity of St. Louis. We do not know what he was doing. But in November 1815 he suddenly appeared in the diary of Jules de Mun, a trader, who was working his way to the headwaters of the Arkansas River and the land of the Arapahos. The partner of de Mun was A. P. Chouteau, one of the distinguished Chouteaus of St. Louis.

The traders were on a dangerous journey. Water was scarce, Indians were plentiful and often hostile. Since the

A grain elevator in the Arkansas Valley, where Greenwood trapped.

government of Spain claimed most of the land southwest of the Arkansas River, trappers and traders were considered trespassers. Any who were caught risked imprisonment and loss of their merchandise. But there was money to be made from the Indians, and the North Americans were willing to gamble.

By the end of November, de Mun and Chouteau had

26

crossed the present Kansas-Colorado border. The mighty Rockies loomed ahead like faint clouds on the horizon. On November 27 the party made camp by the river, and de Mun wrote in his diary:

> One of our men found on the banks of the river two traps suspended from a tree and saw fresh footprints. We sent two men to reconnoitre; they had not yet returned when we saw approaching us on the opposite bank of the river two men who we judged belonged to the party of Americans whose camps we had already seen; this proved to be the case. It was a man named Greenwood and one of his companions. When they had reached the river, and after making some inquiries, we invited them to cross.

Greenwood and his companion explained that with two other men, they had left St. Louis on September 7 to hunt along one of the forks of the Arkansas. But they had seen traces of three other Americans who had apparently been killed by the Pawnees, so they moved on to the main river. Greenwood asked if his men might join the de Mun-Chouteau party. The partners consented. The traders and hunters then continued west through a wilderness where today the tracks of the Santa Fe and Missouri Pacific railroads follow the Arkansas to Pueblo, Colorado.

At the junction of the Arkansas and Huerfano rivers, a rendezvous had been arranged with the men of another trader, whose furs and supplies had been bought by the partners. There was nobody at the appointed place. Friendly Indians told the newcomers that the other party had gone to the Spaniards in search of food. De Mun took off for Taos, more than 150 miles south, to find the missing men. They were there, and happily reported that they had been treated well by the Spaniards.

Returning to the Huerfano with his party, de Mun was ready to start back for St. Louis. So was Greenwood, who had probably spent most of his time hunting. The expedi-

St. Louis in 1832, a booming city, as painted by George Catlin.

tion left on February 27, 1816. It was a rugged trip of 46 days, with little meat, no salt and a constant fear of Indians.

Greenwood and his companions evidently traveled ahead of de Mun and Chouteau. On March 20 the partners caught up with them at an Osage village. Greenwood said they had met a party of Pawnees who had taken their rifles and everything else worth stealing. For 18 days they had walked to reach the Osage settlement, living on nothing but roots. De Mun fed the hunters a supper of cornmeal and water, and in the morning gave them a breakfast of cornmeal and water. After a long diet of roots, the cornmeal must have tasted almost as good as venison.

5
The Life
of a Mountain Man

WHEN CALEB GREENWOOD NEXT APPEARED in the records, for the year 1822, he was unmistakably a mountain man. The mountain men made their living out of the wilderness, generally by trapping. They were as tough as their wrought-iron traps. They could withstand almost any hardship, and this toughness often saved the lives of their companions as well as their own.

One famous mountain man, Hugh Glass, was mauled by a grizzly that tore off part of his flesh and fed it to her cubs. His companions killed the bear and abandoned Glass as practically dead. But the mountain man came to life on a diet of spring water and wild berries. He made up his mind to crawl to Fort Kiowa on the Missouri River, a distance of 100 miles. Glass had one piece of luck: He was able to drive a pack of wolves away from a buffalo calf they had killed, and he carried some of the raw meat with him. He reached the fort.

Another intrepid mountain man was John Colter, a veteran of the Lewis and Clark expedition, who had stayed near the headwaters of the Missouri to trap beaver. He was the first white to see the headwaters of the Colorado, the Teton Mountains, and what is now Yellowstone Park.

One spring morning, while trapping in the area north-west of Yellowstone Park, Colter and a companion were surprised by a party of some 500 Indians. The other trapper shot an Indian and was instantly riddled with arrows. Colter was seized and stripped, then left standing naked while the tribesmen discussed how to kill him. The chief decided to let the white man run for his life, confident of the outcome. Ordering his warriors to stand still, he led Colter out into the prairie 300 or 400 yards and released him. A fierce whoop went up as the Blackfeet took off in pursuit.

Colter was an excellent runner. Desperate, he had no time to dodge the cactus in the open prairie, and his bare feet were soon pierced with thorns. The frantic pace burst some of his blood vessels; blood streamed from his nose and reddened his chest. But after five miles he had outrun all of the Indians except one who, spear in hand, was closing in. Colter suddenly wheeled, surprising his pursuer, who stumbled and fell. The Indian's spear broke in his hand. Colter grabbed the pointed end and thrust it through his pursuer's body, pinning him to the ground. Then he ran for the Jefferson Fork of the Missouri, a mile ahead. Behind him he heard the yells of the Indians when they discovered the body of their comrade.

Nearly fainting, Colter reached the cottonwood trees along the river and plunged into the water. Just downstream there was an island. Spring floods had piled tree trunks and debris against its upper end, making a huge raft. Colter dived under the raft and finally found a place where he could keep his head above water. Sticks and brush piled on top of the tree trunks hid him from view.

A few moments later the Indians came, screeching and yelling "like so many devils," as Colter put it. They swam to the island and climbed over the raft, searching for the fugitive. The mountain man thought he was safe until it

The Indian bread-root, which saved John Colter from the Indians.

occurred to him that the Blackfeet might set fire to the raft. But the Indians at last gave up the search. When night came, Colter swam from his hideaway into the main stream. He went down the river for some distance, being careful not to make any splashes. Then he left the water and traveled all night on his bleeding feet.

At daybreak he felt lucky to be alive. But he knew he was about 250 miles from the nearest outpost, which was Manuel Lisa's fort at the junction of the Big Horn and Yellowstone Rivers. That meant at least a week of walking with no protection from the blistering sun, no moccasins for his thorn-pierced feet, no gun to provide a meal. Any ordinary man would have struggled for a day or two and then given up. The mountain men were not ordinary. Col-

31

ter reached the fort in seven days. He had used broken sticks to dig his daily bread; the root of the plant *Psoralea esculenta,* commonly called the prairie apple, the prairie turnip and the Indian bread-root. Long known to the Indians, this member of the pea family has a starchy, egg-size root, which can be eaten raw, roasted or dried.

A mountain man was not the type to make a pretty girl swoon with joy. His beard was long and dirty, and his hair hung down to his shoulders. He rarely used soap and water, but his face and hands were so burned by the sun that the dirt hardly showed. His buckskin jacket and trousers were stiff with grease and dried blood.

The tools of his trade were five or six traps, a rifle, a knife, a hatchet, a pistol, a powder horn, a bullet mold. All these he carried on him. His stock of coffee, sugar, extra powder and lead, flints, blankets, canvas and a few other supplies were carried on one or two pack horses. After several months in the wilderness, living like an Indian on the animals he shot or trapped, he would load his horses with bales of skins and head for a trading post.

The catch of a good season might be worth $2,000 or more, but the mountain men did not squirrel away their money. Most of it was quickly spent at the trading post. Carefree and reckless after his lonely months, the trapper bought all the whisky he could hold. He gave presents to Indian girls and Mexican senoritas. He bet on pony races and card games and fist fights. Sometimes he had to borrow money for the powder, lead and other supplies he needed for his return to beaver country.

Although some mountain men worked on salary for the big fur companies, those who made history were the free trappers. They roamed where they wished and sold where they could get the best price. In later years, they became the guides for government exploring expeditions and military campaigns.

Caleb Greenwood was one of this fiercely independent breed. Apparently he led a small party into the upper reaches of the Missouri in 1822. We get news of him from a letter written by Major Benjamin O'Fallon, the federal government's Indian agent for the Missouri area. The agent was angry because Caleb had not bothered to get his permission before going into Indian territory. "The report of the Cheyennes killing six men (Greenwood & party) is false, and I am sorry for it," he wrote to a trader. O'Fallon evidently thought that those who ignored the federal regulations should be scalped, but Greenwood had a different notion. He never let an Indian knife touch his head.

By 1822, Caleb was 59, and he was already being called Old Greenwood. He was probably connected with the fur company organized by William H. Ashley and Andrew Henry. This company used free trappers, agreeing to pay them $3 for each pound of beaver fur, or about $5 a skin. A mountain man who dealt with Ashley & Henry was on his own. That was Old Greenwood's way of life.

The next few years were rough. There is no record of Caleb's travels, but it seems likely that he trapped on the Powder River, a branch of the Yellowstone, during the winter of 1822-1823. The Arikara and Blackfeet Indians gave the white men a murderous welcome. Ashley lost 15 men in a sunrise attack. But the friendly Crow tribe provided horses to replace those stolen by other tribes.

The American trappers scored one important victory without firing a shot. A party that undoubtedly included Old Greenwood had reached Bear Lake (on the Utah-Idaho boundary) and followed Bear River first north and then south where the river makes a huge loop on its journey to the Great Salt Lake. In the spring of 1825 the men were camped in the valley of the Great Salt Lake, probably at the mouth of Weber Canyon, a few miles south of the present city of Ogden.

To this area came a rival British trapping expedition led by Peter Skene Ogden of the Hudson's Bay Company— the man for whom the city was named when the Mormons founded it in 1847. When the Americans learned from Jedediah Smith, the great mountain man, that the British were a few miles up Weber Canyon, they leaped on their horses and headed up the canyon. Someone had brought a 20-starred United States flag into the wilds, and this banner was carried to a spot 100 yards from the Hudson's Bay camp. There the Americans set up their own camp.

Ogden was warned that he was on United States territory. His trappers, who had been treated poorly by the Hudson's Bay Company, were invited to join the Americans and make more money. Most of them promptly deserted Ogden, taking their beaver skins with them.

Ogden didn't know that he was actually in Mexico, 50 miles south of the United States border (the 42nd parallel) set by the treaty of 1819. Probably the Americans didn't know it, either, but they had more men and a better price scale. Fearing that he might lose the rest of his men to the jubilant Americans, Ogden quickly turned north to the Snake River country.

In the same spring of 1825 a mountain man rode into the Great Salt Lake country, seeking the camps of trappers. He was Zacharias Ham, one of Ashley's lieutenants. Ham brought news: General Ashley was in the west with fresh supplies of powder, lead and other merchandise needed by the mountain men. He would meet them for trading on July 1 in a meadow by Henry's Fork of the Green River, just north of the Uinta Mountains.

All of the American trappers headed for this, the first rendezvous in the history of the fur trade. They followed Indian trails, forded rivers and reached the meadow, some 100 miles east of Ogden. It is still a lonely spot, bypassed by railroads and national highways, but with a state road

Weber Canyon, where the Americans chased the British from Mexico.

serving the two nearby settlements, Burntfork and Lonetree, Wyoming.

The rendezvous is believed to have been held where the stream called Burntfork joins Henry's Fork. Don Stoll, who today lives on the west side of the highway, says the spot is across the road on the ranch of Orson Behunin. Mr. Stoll's great-grandfather was the first white settler of the area, in 1868.

My wife and I started to walk through the meadow but Mr. Behunin soon overtook us in his pickup truck and drove us about a quarter-mile to the site. A small pile of stones, overgrown with weeds, had once been the chimney of a pioneer's cabin. The country still abounds with wildlife. Only a few years before our visit in 1967 a moose and her calf had wintered by Henry's Fork, feeding on willow twigs.

Historians know pretty well what happened at the rendezvous. Mountain men brought their beaver skins to trade for the supplies that had been hauled west from St. Louis. Friendly Indians came, too. Veteran trappers swapped

35

The valley of Henry's Fork, scene of the historic 1825 rendezvous.

tales, sometimes plain and sometimes fancy, with friends they hadn't seen for months or years. The handful of greenhorns listened to the old-timers and began to build their own stock of memories. Tobacco was smoked and chewed, and a few swigs of expensive whisky warmed some very dry throats.

The rendezvous of 1825 and later years offered only a limited stock of merchandise, and it could not match the entertainment to be had in a Mexican town or a frontier settlement. If any ladies were present, they were Indians —a few of them the wives of trappers. But the rendezvous was a market place, usually hundreds of miles closer to beaver country than any town was.

Caleb Greenwood undoubtedly went to the rendezvous

Orson Behunin stands where trappers assembled by Henry's Fork.

in 1825, and he probably was seen at other rendezvous held each summer through 1840. Different meeting places were often picked by the traders. There were six gatherings up the Green River at Fort Bonneville, where Horse Creek empties into the river.

At every rendezvous, trappers compared notes on the best ways to trap the beaver. One of the great engineers of the animal kingdom, the beaver is an expert swimmer but a poor runner and fighter. To protect himself from wolves, coyotes, mountain lions and other enemies, he surrounds his house with water. Streams are dammed to make ponds or even large lakes. The water spreads outward from the banks and into the woods. When beavers gnaw down trees to feed on the inner bark of trunk and branches, they are close to water. Water is the difference between life and death.

Some beavers live in burrows dug into the banks of rivers or large streams. But the best known dwelling is the beaver lodge, a huge structure of small branches and mud built on a beaver-made island in a beaver-made pond. Like the burrow, the lodge always has an entrance under water.

Thanks to this engineering skill, the beaver population flourished. But the beavers could not cope with the mountain men and their iron traps. Thousands of colonies were wiped out as the trappers moved farther and farther into the wilderness. There was some risk that the beaver might become as rare as the buffalo is today, or might disappear entirely—as happened in Europe.

What saved the beaver was a change in fashion. Silk hats became popular, and beaver hats went out of style. The traders brought the bad news to the mountain men: Beaver fur was worth only a third or a quarter of what it used to bring. So the trappers went after other animals, or gave up the hunt to start ranching in a mountain-rimmed valley of the west. Choosing homesteads where a stream flowed gently through a lush green meadow, few of the trappers understood how the level meadow had developed in a rocky canyon. Over hundreds of years the deep, rich soil had washed down from the hillsides and piled up behind ancient beaver dams. Had it not been for beavers, there would have been scant pasture for the mountain man's cattle, no fields for his wheat.

6
Caleb Takes a Wife

OLD GREENWOOD CAME TO GENERAL ASHLEY'S rendezvous of 1825 with 202 pounds of beaver skins, probably the catch of two years. The General's account book
shows they were bought for $3 a pound, or $606. Greenwood used part of the money to buy a pistol for $45 and
1½ pounds of coffee and 1½ pounds of sugar, each selling
for $1.50 a pound.

The day after the rendezvous, Ashley started for St. Louis
with 25 men and a number of pack horses. Greenwood was
no doubt one of the escorts for this fur caravan. The General's plan was to ride north to the head of navigation on
the Big Horn River, transfer to boats, follow the Big Horn
to the Yellowstone River and thus reach the Missouri River
at the western boundary of present North Dakota. The long
journey down the Missouri to St. Louis would have threats
from Indians as well as perils of navigation, but it would
be safer than the shorter route overland. Further, the pack
horses could be returned to the trappers, who needed the
animals.

Twice on the five-week pack trip to the Big Horn, the
Ashley party was attacked, once by Blackfeet and once by
Crows. Most of the horses were stampeded and captured
by screaming Indians, but no one in the trading party was
killed.

Greenwood probably left General Ashley at the Big Horn

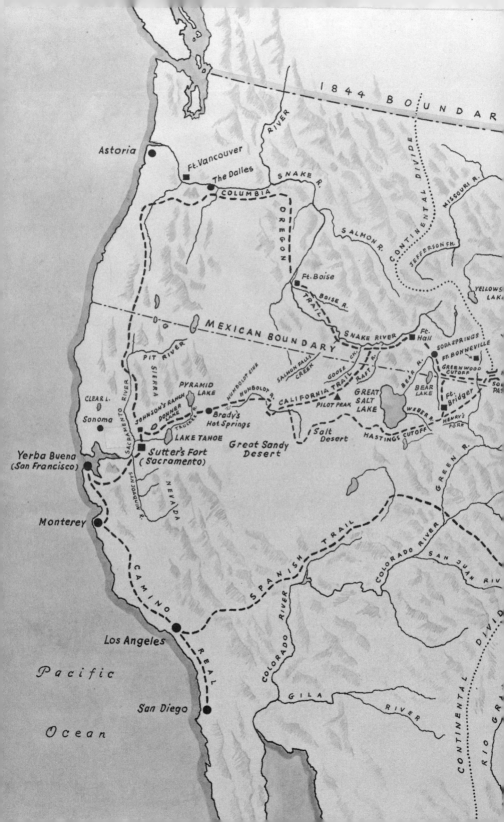

and headed eastward through the Platte Valley. He may have had one or two companions, for traveling alone was risky. All we are sure of is that on November 26 he reached Fort Atkinson on the Missouri, near the site of Omaha. James Kennerly, who sold provisions at the fort, noted in his diary that day, "Greenwood come from the mountains." Three weeks later the diary reported that Greenwood had bought a horse for $95 from an army sergeant, and the last mention of Caleb was on December 22, 1825. On that day Kennerly said Greenwood "with his fine horse" took off for the Sioux country with one of the partners of the French Fur Company. The Sioux were spread over a vast area of the upper Missouri Valley and westward into the Rockies.

Caleb evidently rode through the Sioux country and into the territory of the Crows, the long-time enemies of the Sioux. The Crows were settled around the Yellowstone River in Montana. And it was somewhere in this area, not long after he left Fort Atkinson, that Caleb picked a young Crow woman as his wife.

Nothing is known of the romance. The old mountain man, who had never married, was then 62 or 63. He probably carried a stock of beads or other trinkets that pleased the dark-haired young woman, who was most likely in her twenties. He could speak enough of her language to excite her with tales of his adventures, and perhaps with tales of adventures he had only dreamed of. No doubt she admired his fine horse.

The name of the bride was, according to family tradition, Batchicka Youngcault. She was believed to be half-French, probably the daughter of one of the French pioneers in the fur trade.

We do not know where or how Mr. and Mrs. Greenwood lived. No visitor left any record that has been discovered so far, and neither Caleb nor Batchicka could write. The couple may have lived with the Crow Indians for a while,

CROW INDIANER   INDIENS CORBEAUX.

CROW INDIANS

Crow Indians, from an aquatint made by Karl Bodmer in 1840.

but sooner or later Caleb's independent spirit would have pushed him to a life of his own.

Old Greenwood used to speak with contempt of some Indians, but he had deep admiration for the Crows. Batchicka strengthened his admiration. Once, after a desert trip, Caleb's eyes were in bad condition. His wife insisted that he go to a doctor in St. Louis, a trip of more than 2,000 miles down the Yellowstone and Missouri rivers. She herself paddled the canoe.

43

As they were passing an Indian village, the canoe was noticed and pulled ashore. The Indians began helping themselves to the provisions. "Let them take everything," Old Greenwood said, "and maybe they will let us pass." Batchicka had hidden a kettle of meat under her skirt. When an Indian discovered it and reached for it, the Crow woman lost her temper. She hit the brave over the head with her paddle, knocking him into the river. The Indians gathered on the shore roared with delight. "Heap brave squaw!" they shouted. As a reward, they put everything back in the boat and sent the couple on their way.

The St. Louis doctor helped to restore Caleb's sight, and Batchicka then encouraged her husband to try farming in the Missouri Valley. But the old mountain man was not cut out to be a successful farmer. He belonged to the distant mountains and deserts, the winds and the stars. His hands were better molded to his rifle than to the handles of a plow, and he was more comfortable in the saddle than on a wagon seat.

Caleb and Batchicka lost no time in starting a family. Their first child was probably John, born about 1827. There were four more sons: Britton Bailey, Governor Boggs, William Sublette and James Case. One daughter was named Angeline and a second daughter, Sarah Mojave, came in 1843 when Caleb was 80 years old.

Batchicka died a few months after the birth of Sarah Mojave. The family tradition is that she was buried in St. Louis. Caleb's 17 years of married life were finished, and he was once more on his own. It is not clear how his youngest children were raised, or how he kept in touch with them. Probably they were turned over to friends or to some of Batchicka's relatives. What we do know is that in 1844 Greenwood turned again toward the west, guiding a party of emigrants. Some of his most exciting years were still ahead of him at age 81.

44

7

First Wagons
Across the Sierra

THE FAR WEST MADE IMAGINATIONS dance in the early 1800s. Little was known about the Pacific slope, although trappers, fur traders, explorers and missionaries had gone to the Oregon country and to California. In 1840 there was a turning point. A family started out from Missouri for Oregon, not to collect skins or souls, but simply to live there. Joel Walker, the head of the family, was a brother of the famous Joseph Reddeford Walker of Virginia, fur hunter and mountain man. Joseph Walker had made history in 1833 and 1834 by blazing what became known as the California Trail, following the Humboldt River west to the Sierra Nevada.

There was no road for these pioneers. They traveled by horse and boat and sometimes on foot. Most of those who headed west after Joel Walker were bound for Oregon. They were suspicious of California, which was part of Mexico.

In 1841, however, the Bartleson party of 31 men, one woman and her child struck out for California and got there. They had to abandon their wagons near the present Utah-Nevada line and pack the rest of the way, but they proved that the route was possible. Still, as the emigrants increased

Alfalfa, corn, and a Union Pacific mixed train on the North Platte.

during the next few years from a handful to a multitude, Oregon was the overwhelming choice.

A stout group of Missourians from the area of Kansas City decided in 1844 to seek their fortunes in California. They picked Council Bluffs, Iowa, across the Missouri from Omaha, as their starting point. It was a lucky choice, for floods delayed the emigrants gathered farther down the Missouri at Independence and St. Joseph.

The caravan of 27 wagons with about 40 men and a number of women left Council Bluffs near the end of May. One of the emigrants was 18-year-old Moses Schallenberger, who wrote a report on the journey 40 years later. Thanks to him, we know that Caleb Greenwood was hired to guide the party from the Missouri to the Rockies. Caleb's two eldest sons, John and Britton, rode with their father.

This pioneer wagon train to California has become known as the Stephens-Townsend-Murphy party. Elisha Stephens,

46

who was elected captain, was a blacksmith from South Carolina. He had worked for the Indian agency at Council Bluffs. Dr. John Townsend was a gentle physician from the neighborhood of Wheeling, West Virginia. Martin Murphy was a political refugee from Ireland, whose wife and three granddaughters had died from malaria in Missouri. He wanted to get away from the deadly region, and when a Jesuit missionary described the glorious climate and fertile soil of California, he made up his mind. He was not much concerned about the Mexicans. The missionary had assured him that the cross was planted on every hillside and in every valley, which was certainly not the case in Missouri.

Old Greenwood led the company along the Platte River to the North Platte, bordered by willows and giant cottonwoods that formed a ribbon of dark green through the sagebrush hills and bluffs. Today the valley has irrigated fields of lush alfalfa and corn. Millions of grasshoppers revel in the transformation, and thousands of seagulls revel among the grasshoppers. "They eat grasshoppers until their craws are stuffed and then they throw up and start eating again," one rancher said.

After traveling some 400 miles from Council Bluffs the emigrants passed the first towering landmark, Chimney Rock, on the south side of the river. Rising from a hill about 300 feet high, the rock itself stood 200 feet in the 1840s, but it has eroded to about 150 feet today.

The party was badly worried about Indians. Although the Otos and Pawnees had caused no trouble, what would happen when the train entered the country of the warlike Sioux? The answer came 90 miles past Chimney Rock as the emigrants reached Fort Laramie at the end of June. Encamped around the fort were about 4,000 Sioux, including squaws and children. Old Greenwood took one look and declared there would be no attack so long as the warriors' families were with them. He was right.

Chimney Rock, landmark of the emigrants, on the North Platte River.

Several days were spent at Fort Laramie so the animals could enjoy a rest and good pasture. Some of the horses were traded for tough Indian ponies, and moccasins were bought to replace shoes and boots that had been badly worn.

Striking camp, the company followed the North Platte farther west, passing the site of Casper, and then headed for Independence Rock, the great landmark of the Sweetwater River. Captain Stephens ordered that the wagons keep close together so they could be quickly formed into a corral in case of attack. There were few rifles among the Indians in those days, and the emigrants believed they could repulse an attack made with arrows.

Independence Rock, rising 155 feet above the river, is a vast boulder covering 27 acres. It was a welcome sight to the emigrants because it marked the end of the alkaline water of the North Platte and a good drink from the Sweetwater, a gentle stream barely 20 feet wide. Passing travelers carved some 5,000 names on the rock, which became known as "the great register of the desert." The name "Independence" was given when a band of hunters camped

48

Above: At Independence Rock, pioneers drank from Sweetwater River.

Below: Cliff swallows build nests on Independence Rock.

49

Across the Sweetwater to South Pass (right, marked by snow fences).

at the base of the rock one Fourth of July and celebrated the holiday with stone carving.

Most of the old names have worn away but some replacements have been provided by 20th century visitors using paint instead of chisels. Wild roses still bloom in the grass at the base of the rock, and cottontails lope along the steep shoulder with the sureness of lizards.

A little more than 100 miles west of Independence Rock, the company wound its way through canyons and up mountain slopes to South Pass, the most famous crossing of the Continental Divide. The view from the summit was just the opposite of what a pass is supposed to be. Instead of finding a rocky gap and a steep descent, the emigrants saw

At South Pass, remnants of the old Oregon Trail are still visible.

a broad and almost level plain that faded into the haze of the horizon. It was hard to tell exactly where the Atlantic watershed ended and the Pacific watershed began. The discoverer of the pass is unknown, but it was probably Etienne Provost, one of Old Greenwood's fellow trappers at the first rendezvous in 1825.

As early as 1827 a cannon on a mule-drawn carriage had been hauled through South Pass to defend General Ashley's fur business at Bear Lake. When Greenwood led the emigrants through in 1844, the route was already well marked by the wagon wheels of parties bound for Oregon. Today some remnants of the Oregon Trail, used as a highway in later years, may still be seen from State Highway 28 or

The old schoolhouse and the milk house, restored, at Fort Bridger.

followed on foot. Not until 1963 was a railroad built through the pass. The United States Steel Company constructed the line to carry iron from a huge open pit mine east of the Continental Divide to the Union Pacific's main line at Rock Springs, Wyoming.

Twenty miles beyond South Pass the Stephens-Townsend-Murphy party blazed a new trail which for a time was known as the Greenwood Cutoff. The old trail, avoiding a desert, swung southwest to Fort Bridger, then turned northwest to Bear Lake and the Bear River. Greenwood and another veteran of the mountains, Isaac Hitchcock, were apparently anxious to save two or three days' travel by going directly west across the unexplored desert. It was a dangerous gamble, made all the more risky because Hitchcock estimated the distance to Green River at only 25 miles (actually it was at least 50). The emigrants failed to carry water from the Big Sandy when they left their encampment at daybreak on a July morning. Soon the sun was scorching the rough land and the meager supply of water was used up. No spring was found; there was no sign of Green River when the travelers were forced by darkness to make camp. During the night about 40 head of cattle, crazed by thirst, broke away and ran off in search of water.

With the first light of day, the weary emigrants pushed on, and by 11 a.m. they reached the Green River about five miles south of the present La Barge. People and animals drank their fill and rested. Most of the stray cows were found.

The wagon train probably left the river through a narrow dry gulch on the west shore. There are smooth sandstone walls on each side, and on them may still be seen the names of hundreds of emigrants who later used the Greenwood Cutoff. The place has become known as Names Hill.

Old Greenwood's party had 40 miles of travel from Green River to the Bear River at present Cokeville, Wyoming, where they rejoined the Oregon Trail. It was rough and mountainous country, but there was no lack of water and grass.

Later the shortcut was renamed Sublette's Cutoff after the famous mountain man, Solomon P. Sublette. Some of the Forty-niners had their wagons wrecked on the desert when the thirsty oxen stampeded at the smell of Green River ahead. Charles Kelly has proposed that Old Greenwood's role be remembered by calling the parched land between the Big Sandy and Green River the Greenwood Desert. No desert ever had such a verdant name.

The Oregon Trail followed the Bear River to Soda Springs, where Old Greenwood's party gaped at a variety of hot springs. One of them, like Old Faithful in Yellowstone Park, erupted at regular intervals—but the hot fountain rose only three feet. The present town was founded by a group of Mormons who had broken away from the church.

A few miles west of Soda Springs, the Bear River turns from a northbound course to a southbound route to Great Salt Lake. Old Greenwood led the company away from Bear River and across a divide to the Portneuf River, one of the tributaries of the Snake River. The Portneuf was followed to Fort Hall on the Snake.

Fort Hall was the most important station on the Oregon Trail. Here the emigrants rested for several days, making repairs and buying a few supplies at fancy prices. Then they moved on 50 miles west to Raft River, where the California Trail turned off from the Oregon Trail. It was a place of decision. How many would go to California, how many to Oregon? Sixteen wagons stayed on the Oregon Trail and 11 turned toward California, with about 41 persons. The date was probably September 1, 1844.

Not even Old Greenwood felt sure of the trail to California, which had been pioneered by Joseph Reddeford Walker. The first wagons had followed it to the foot of the Sierra only the year before. But the company managed to push through rough country to the headwaters of the Humboldt River near the present Wells, Nevada. For 300 miles the river, a sure source of water and grass, was followed through the desert. Hundreds of Indians gathered at the camp every night. Schallenberger called them "indolent and degraded . . . totally without energy." But if they were not models of American enterprise, at least they were friendly.

When the party reached the Humboldt Sink, where the river disappeared into the sands of the desert, there was an argument over the best route to California. Some of the emigrants wanted to turn south; others favored a course

54

Above: An osprey's nest on Big Sandy, south of the Greenwood Cutoff.

Below: The Green River—water after crossing the Greenwood Desert.

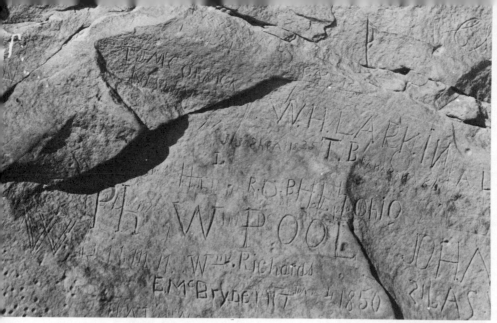

A part of Names Hill on the Green River. Carving began in 1844.

due west. Discussions went on for a week while the oxen rested and everybody complained about the alkali in the water. Schallenberger tells the outcome:

> Finally, an old Indian was found, called Truckee, with whom Old Man Greenwood talked by means of signs and diagrams drawn on the ground. From him it was learned that 50 or 60 miles to the west there was a river that flowed easterly from the mountains, and that along this stream there were large trees and good grass. Acting on this information, Dr. Townsend, Captain Stephens, and Joseph Foster, taking Truckee as a guide, started out to explore this route, and after three days returned, reporting that they had found the river just as the Indian had described it.

The river, which flows from Lake Tahoe through Reno to Pyramid Lake, was named for the Indian who may have saved the lives of the company.

Truckee was the father of Chief Winnemucca and the grandfather of Sarah Winnemucca Hopkins, who wrote

Life Among the Piutes in 1883. The granddaughter explained that Truckee was a nickname given by Old Greenwood's fellow-travelers because the old chief, always trying
to please, would answer "truckee" to nearly any question
asked. In his language, "truckee" meant "OK."

The emigrants left the Humboldt Sink around October
15 after cooking two days' rations and filling every available
keg and kettle with water. This was the first wagon train
to cross the Forty-Mile Desert. Many thousands of other
emigrants would feel the blast of the dusty route until the
first transcontinental railroad was opened in 1869.

Schallenberger said the trail was "knee deep in alkali
dust," a pardonable exaggeration. There was enough water
for the people, but not enough for the oxen. At the present
Brady's Hot Springs, halfway to the Truckee River, water
was dipped from the springs and allowed to cool in tubs
for the cattle—which became sick after drinking. Having
had no food and practically no water for two days, the oxen
were in bad shape as the company neared the river. An
order was issued to unhitch the animals, lest they stampede
and wreck the wagons. As soon as they were free the oxen
galloped for the river.

The wagon train rested at the Truckee for two days while
the oxen regained their strength from the abundant grass.
Old Greenwood knew that snow would soon be deep on
the ground, and the Sierra Nevada range must be crossed
before the party was trapped. Indeed, it is likely that the
first light snow came a day or two after the company began
moving up the Truckee River toward Donner Lake.

The route became extremely difficult after the first few
days. The twisting canyon narrowed ("the hills began to
grow nearer together" was the way Schallenberger described
the change). The river was so crooked that the wagons had
to keep crossing from one bank to another. Once there were
ten crossings in a single mile. Finally there was no room

on the steep slopes for the wagons, and the only passage was in the stony bed of the shallow river. The water softened the hooves of the oxen, which then became badly bruised by the stones. The beasts refused to move unless the drivers walked beside them in the river, goading them on. Often it was necessary to hitch up three teams to pull a single wagon. Progress was painfully and dangerously slow.

Worst of all, a foot of snow fell, burying the grass on which the oxen depended. The hungry beasts would bawl all night long after a hard day's work. The emigrants fed them twigs of pine needles, but this was poor fare. Then the party reached a stand of rushes that had not been buried by the snow. The ravenous oxen ate so greedily that two animals died. Afterward, scouts were sent ahead each day to find the next patch of rushes and locate a camp for the night. Although the rushes were not so nourishing as grass, they kept the cattle alive, and the men took care that the animals did not overeat.

After about three weeks of exhausting travel along the river, averaging barely four miles a day, the train reached the site of the present town of Truckee, California. Here the river forked, with the main stream turning southwest and the tributary continuing due west. Which should be followed?

The tributary looked better for wagons, but the main stream might offer a better route for horses. So the party divided. Four men and two women set off on horseback, with two pack horses, toward the southwest. This group came to the shore of Lake Tahoe—probably the first white persons ever to reach this deep lake, more than a mile above sea level, which Fremont had seen from a distance nine months earlier. The riders followed the west shore of the lake and then braved the steep slopes of the towering Sierra.

The horses made the climb, crossed the summit, and then carried their riders down the western slope to the American

The Portneuf River, on Greenwood's trail, boils toward the Snake.

River and the Sacramento Valley. Fortunately, there was little snow on the western slope, and plenty of meat was provided by John and Dan Murphy, who were excellent hunters. Three weeks after separating from the wagon train, the party reached Sinclair's Ranch on the American River. After several days' rest, the riders went a few miles down the river to Sutter's Fort, arriving about December 10. They got a warm welcome from John Sutter, the always hospitable Swiss who had emigrated to the United States only 10 years earlier.

59

Old Greenwood and his two sons stayed with the wagon train. The company followed the tributary (Donner Creek) two and one-half miles to Donner Lake. Only one mountain separated the travelers from California, but this mountain was not friendly to emigrants with wagons. After several days of exploring for a pass, the leaders picked the route near today's Southern Pacific Railroad and Interstate 80. The oxen were so worn out, however, that half of the party abandoned their wagons and took only the supplies they could pack.

The snow was then about two feet deep, and it was impossible for the weakened oxen to pull loaded wagons. So the wagons were unloaded and everything was carried uphill. Then the teams were doubled to haul the empty wagons. But the travelers soon faced a more frightening obstacle, as told by Schallenberger:

> When about half way up the mountain they came to a vertical rock about ten feet high. It seemed now that everything would have to be abandoned except what the men could carry on their backs. After a tedious search they found a rift in the rock, just about wide enough to let one ox pass at a time. Removing the yokes from the cattle, they managed to get them one by one through this chasm to the top of the rock. There the yokes were replaced, chains were fastened to the tongues of the wagons, and carried to the top of the rock, where the cattle were hitched to them. Then the men lifted at the wagons, while the cattle pulled at the chains, and by this ingenious device the vehicles were all, one by one, got across the barrier.

To accomplish this feat in good weather, with dry ground, would have been difficult. To accomplish it in two feet of snow seems miraculous. "Nowhere else," Charles Kelly and Dale Morgan say, "in all his years in the West, had Old Greenwood had to contend with a pass like this."

Twenty miles west of the summit the company came to

Beside the Humboldt River west of Elko, a magpie poses on a cable.

the headwaters of the Yuba River and made camp. Seventeen able-bodied men set out on foot for Sutter's Fort, driving the cattle and expecting to make a prompt return with supplies for the 15 or so persons left behind. Old Greenwood and his sons traveled with the forward party, which reached Sutter's Fort about three days after the mounted party that had traveled by way of Lake Tahoe. Sutter was delighted to see these North Americans, for there was serious political trouble brewing in California and the Swiss pioneer had decided to lead a small army south. He enrolled Caleb and his two sons, Martin Murphy and his five sons, Stephens and two other men. Dr. Townsend was recruited as staff surgeon, but he had no bullet wounds to dress because the rule of warfare in California was strictly observed: All shooting was done while the opposing forces

61

Interstate 80 sweeps over Truckee River and the Southern Pacific.

were out of range. The campaign, called the Micheltorena War after the last Mexican governor, ended in a surrender near Los Angeles on February 21, 1845. Sutter was held prisoner for about a month.

Meanwhile, two sections of the Stephens-Townsend-Murphy party were still in the mountains. In addition to the group of 15 at the head of the Yuba River, young Schallenberger was alone in a cabin at Donner Lake. He and two men, Joseph Foster and Allen Montgomery, had been guarding supplies that could not be hauled over Donner Pass. Two wornout cows had been left for provisions, and the men had quickly built themselves a rude cabin. They did not expect the snow to get deeper than two feet; further, fresh animals would soon come from Sutter's, enabling them to complete the trip.

The night their cabin was finished, three feet of snow fell. By the end of the week the cabin was nearly covered. The three decided to leave on makeshift snowshoes while they could still get out. After an exhausting struggle to the summit, eighteen-year-old Moses Schallenberger could not go farther. He followed the tracks back to the cabin where, miraculously, he lived through the winter by trapping foxes. The two men reached the Sacramento Valley safely.

The snowbound emigrants in the mountains had not been forgot by Sutter. While riding south with his troops, he had sent an order back to the fort, directing that horses, supplies and Indians be provided for a rescue. But Dennis Martin, a Canadian and one of the original company who had gone ahead with Old Greenwood, was the first to reach the camp on the Yuba. He traveled on snowshoes. Everybody was alive, but not exactly well fed. One woman and her children had lived two weeks on boiled rawhide.

Martin distributed the food he carried on his back and then pushed on across the summit and down to Donner Lake in search of Moses Schallenberger, who had been alone for three months. Schallenberger describes his arrival:

One evening a little before sunset, about the last of February, as I was standing a short distance from my cabin, I thought I could distinguish the form of a man moving towards me. I first thought it was an Indian, but very soon I recognized the familiar face of Dennis Martin. My feelings can be better imagined than described.

Looking up along the Donner Pass route of the first wagon train.

Martin showed young Moses how to fix his crude snow-shoes so he could travel with less than half the labor, but the lad was weak from lack of food and exercise. The two managed, however, to get back to the camp on the Yuba, where a daughter had just been born to Mr. and Mrs. Martin Murphy.

Another blessed event was the arrival of a pack train from Fort Sutter. Everybody ate heartily, and then the party started for the Sacramento Valley. Some had saddles, some used pack saddles and some rode bareback—but nobody walked. That night the travelers camped on the banks of the flooded Bear River. It was March 1, 1845, just a year since they had left their homes in Missouri. After some days the water level of the river fell enough to permit a crossing and the party continued to the Feather River, where Captain Sutter had a boat waiting to ferry them across. Best of all, the vaqueros provided a fat cow which was roasted for the first square meal in months.

At Sutter's Fort the Stephens-Townsend-Murphy party disbanded after its historic crossing of the Sierra. The various families and individuals sought their fortunes in different ways and different places.

Caleb and his two sons went north after the collapse of the Micheltorena War. Their next trip would be east across the Sierra Nevada.

[For a map of the two routes of the Stephens-Townsend-Murphy party across the Sierra Nevada, see page 105.]

8

Return Trip

P ARTIES TRAVELING FROM CALIFORNIA to the United
States used to take the Spanish Trail, which was a long
way around through the South. Now that a new route had
been blazed westward through Donner Pass to Sutter's Fort,
the same route could be used for eastern travel. And Caleb
Greenwood reappears as guide for an eastbound party that
left Sutter's on May 12, 1845, heading for Fort Hall on
the Snake River. Again, John and Britton rode with their
father, who was then 82 years old.

Old Greenwood may have hoped that friends or relatives
would have brought his youngest children as far west as
Fort Hall. In any event, he could earn money as guide
for the eastbound party and collect another fee for leading
a second company of emigrants west. And it may have
been that his experience as pilot for the first wagon train
to cross the Sierra left a deep imprint. Old Greenwood
was the pathfinder, and he probably took pride in the trail
he blazed. Yet he would always be on the lookout for better
routes, such as a way to avoid that difficult journey up the
Truckee River.

There were a dozen in the eastbound party, not counting
the Greenwoods. One was William H. Winter, who kept
a journal that brings the trip to life. The horsemen went
up the Bear River to its source in a large marsh, high above
the Sacramento Valley. They crossed to the nearby Yuba

66

River, which was a serious obstacle because of the steep, rocky walls of the canyon and snow that was about four feet deep. They found a place to make camp, after stripping their horses and forcing them into the river, where they swam to an island and stood all night in the snow. The men kindled a huge fire and debated how they could cross the river. First they felled a tree, but the swift stream carried it away. Next they swung their axes into a tall fir, cut it half through and went to bed.

In the morning they toppled the fir, which broke in two. The top was swept away, but the main trunk was held by a boulder in the stream. From the broken end the men were able to throw poles to the shore, forming a bridge.

After a difficult passage up the Yuba, the party reached the base of the mountain ridge. Struggling upward through a forest of granite boulders, the travelers gained the bald summit and "a sudden thrill of joy awakened in every bosom and flashed in every eye"—for the eastern slope was almost free of snow. Far below they could see a green meadow and the blue water of Donner Lake.

Little time was spent in admiring the splendid panorama because the horses were in their third day without food. The travelers hurried down the mountain to the meadow at Donner Lake and stayed there the rest of the day while the animals grazed. Apparently it was John Greenwood who found a route around the north end of the Verdi Range via Dog Valley, for the present Prosser Creek was soon being called John's or John Greenwood's Creek. This route kept the party out of the stony Truckee River canyon.

Winter's journal describes the Indians of the Truckee River as entirely naked and miserably poor. They lived in houses of woven rushes on rafts made from willow brush, and ate lizards, crickets and mussels.

To prepare for the 40-mile journey across the waterless desert from the Truckee River to the sink of the Humboldt

River, the horses were rested for a full day. The desert was crossed successfully, but there was a shortage of grass along the river. Camping one night near the present Elko, the party was astonished to find in the morning that four horses had been shot by Indians who had swum the river in a quest for food. Two of the travelers remained behind, hidden in the brush, to shoot any Indian who approached a dead horse. After two hours an Indian appeared, some 250 yards away. He studied the tracks and then vanished without coming into range for a good shot.

The party left the Humboldt River at its head, swung north and crossed the grassy spur of a mountain. Here the streams ran north toward Snake River through country with excellent grass. Although Winter does not identify it, the Salmon Falls Creek may have been the river they followed to the hot springs of Thousand Springs Valley, near the present Twin Falls, Idaho, on Snake River. Salmon Falls Creek is now the route of the Union Pacific Railroad to Wells, Nevada. Bearing east again, the party crossed the Raft River and arrived June 20, 1845, at Fort Hall on the Snake River, just 39 days after leaving Sutter's.

Winter's report is found in a small book, *Route Across the Rocky Mountains, with a Description of Oregon and California,* published in 1846 with Overton Johnson as co-author. Later he went back to California to live. Although neither Caleb nor his sons are mentioned in the book, much of the route described was theirs.

Like most easterners, Winter was used to forested hills and broad, fertile valleys. He liked the hospitable lands of Oregon and California but saw no future for the rough country he traveled with the Greenwoods. He summed up his opinions with this sour paragraph:

In the whole country between the Eastern base of the California Mountains, and Fort Hall, we saw no game, of any description, excepting a few Antelopes, on the head of

68

Alders hide Salmon Falls Creek in the center of the photograph.

Marie's River [the Humboldt, also known as Mary's]. The greater portion of the country, after leaving the head waters of the Sacramento, is either broken by mountains, or covered with extensive wastes of sand and volcanic desolation; and can never be inhabited, by a people much superior to the insect and reptile eating savages, found at the present time upon some of its streams.

Other travelers and many statesmen made equally bad guesses about the value of the mountains and deserts of the west. Four-lane interstate highways are now linking the towns and cities along Old Greenwood's route, and none of the people eats insects on purpose.

9
California Ho!

THE THREE GREENWOODS SAID GOODBYE to the Winter
party at Fort Hall and waited as guests of Captain
Richard Grant for the overland wagon trains that would
arrive from the east in late July or early August.

Fort Hall had been built in the summer of 1834 by Na-
thaniel J. Wyeth, a remarkably enterprising young man
from Cambridge, Massachusetts, who had hoped to make
a fortune in the fur trade but was defeated by the big fur
companies. He had brought a large quantity of merchandise across the prairies to the 1834 rendezvous on Ham's
Fork of the Green River near the present Kemmerer, Wyoming. The Rocky Mountain Fur Company had contracted
to buy the goods but broke its contract. Wyeth decided to
build his own trading post and fort on the Snake River,
the dark and mighty stream that had sawed a deep channel
through lava beds on its journey to the Columbia.

The fort was named for Henry Hall, one of Wyeth's
financial backers. Construction proceeded so well in the
first three weeks that Wyeth resumed his trip to the Pacific
Coast, leaving 12 men at the garrison. There was a mem-
orable celebration, which Wyeth recalled in a letter to his
uncle, written from the Columbia River two months later:

> We manufactured a magnificent flag from some un-
> bleached sheeting, a little red flannel and a few blue patches;

saluted it with damaged powder and wet it in villainous alcohol, and after all it makes, I do assure you, a very respectable appearance among the dry and desolate regions of central America. Its bastions stand a terror to the skulking Indian and a beacon of safety to the fugitive hunter. It is manned by 12 men and has constantly loaded in the bastions 100 guns and rifles.

Three years later Wyeth, lacking capital to compete with the British, sold Fort Hall to the Hudson's Bay Company, which held it until about 1856. Floods destroyed the ruins in the early 1860s. The site, close by the Snake River on the Fort Hall Indian reservation, was lost in tall grass along a dirt road until a stone marker was erected a century after the fort had disappeared.

When Greenwood was at Fort Hall, the post was the most important on the Overland Trail. It was Caleb's plan to persuade emigrants bound for Oregon to take the California trail instead, and he knew how to do it. Joel Palmer, a member of an Oregon party, described Greenwood as "an old mountaineer, well stocked with falsehoods." No doubt Caleb was a skillful talker, and he may have stretched the truth in his recruiting. He would ride from wagon to wagon as the emigrants sat by their camp fires around Fort Hall. The 82-year-old man with a long white beard, dressed in buckskins, moccasins and fur cap, was a figure to be remembered for the rest of their lives. He would invite everyone to come to a gathering where an important announcement would be made. Curious, all of the emigrants would assemble at the appointed hour, and Old Greenwood would start talking.

The emigrants were warned that if they continued to Oregon they would have to make two crossings of the Snake River and one of the Columbia, and that no company had ever challenged these wild rivers without losing one or more men. They were told that three or four tribes of hostile

Fort Hall, outside and in, drawn by Major Osborne Cross in 1849.

Indians were ready to ambush them. If they got past the Indians, they faced death from starvation in the winter snows of the Cascade Mountains.

On the other hand, the California route was much shorter,

with no threats from vengeful Indians or turbulent rivers. If Old Greenwood did not mention the Forty-Mile Desert from the Humboldt Sink to the Truckee or the exhausting climb to the summit of the Sierra Nevada, he may be pardoned. "He was merely setting a precedent for that particular brand of real estate agent who made California the eighth wonder of the world," Charles Kelly wrote. "Old Greenwood was one of California's first civic boosters."

One of those who heard Caleb's speech was a boy not quite seven, Benjamin Franklin Bonney. Seventy-eight years later, in 1923, he still remembered it:

> After Greenwood had spoken the men of our party held a pow-wow which lasted nearly all night. Some wanted to go to California, while others were against it. Barlow, who was in charge of our train, said that he would forbid any man leaving the train and going to California. He told us we did not know what we were getting into, that there was a great uncertainty about land titles in California, that we were Americans and should not want to go to another country under another flag. Some argued that California would become American territory in time; others thought that Mexico would fight to hold it and that the Americans who went there would get into a mixup and probably get killed.
>
> The meeting broke up in a mutiny. Barlow finally appealed to the men to go to Oregon and make Oregon an American territory and not waste their time going to California to help promote Sutter's land schemes.
>
> Next morning old Caleb Greenwood with his boys stepped out to one side and said: "All you who want to go to California drive out from the main train and follow me. You will find there are no Indians to kill you, the roads are better, and you will be allowed to take up more land in California than in Oregon, the climate is better, there is plenty of hunting and fishing, and the rivers are full of salmon."

The boy's father, Jarvis Bonney, was the first to pull out from the Oregon train to follow Greenwood. Seven other wagons followed, amid such farewells as this: "Goodbye, we will never see you again. Your bones will whiten in the desert or be gnawed by wild animals in the mountains."

Altogether, 10 wagons left Fort Hall with the Greenwoods on August 9, and 15 more joined the train at the Humboldt River. The diary of Jacob R. Snyder tells of their trip down the Snake to Raft River, past the City of Rocks to Goose Creek, and thence over the divide to the Humboldt, which they reached on August 25. Moving down the Humboldt, the company usually made 18 or 20 miles each day. The Snake Indians had been making war on the Diggers, and the emigrants passed several deserted Digger villages, some with unburied bodies.

There was a brief panic in the train when a cloud of dust swept toward it on September 4. Indians were riding up for an attack, the emigrants thought. But the dust cloud was only a whirlwind.

Two days later Snyder's diary reported briefly, "An Indian was shot by young Greenwood this morning. He was discovered concealed in the bushes and immediately shot."

The killing occurred near Winnemucca. Benjamin F. Bonney wrote a detailed account of it long afterward. His version was that John Greenwood was acting as pilot one day when an Indian stood up in the sagebrush, frightening John's horse. The horse reared, John jerked hard and the horse nearly threw him. The young men who were riding alongside laughed, and John declared he would kill the Indian. When he aimed his rifle, the Indian threw up his hands; John's companions told him not to shoot, for the Indian meant no harm. The frightened Indian then ran, and young Greenwood shot him through the back. Benjamin's mother laid the dying Indian on a quilt.

At dusk, Old Greenwood and his other son rode into camp with more wagons. They had found the Indian and shot him through the head to end his suffering. "The man who killed that Indian must die," said Caleb. "Your son John shot him," said Bonney's father. Old Greenwood did not quail. He told the men that anyone who saw John should shoot him on sight.

Bonney's story is doubtful. But it does seem clear that an Indian was wantonly killed by John Greenwood, and that the young man then left the train.

One Indian got the better of a Texan named Sam Kinney, a big man who was feared by everyone. As related by Bonney, the Texan stopped his wagon when he saw the Indian in the sagebrush. He took a pair of handcuffs and started toward the Indian, who did not suspect trouble. Bonney's father asked what he intended to do. "I am going to capture that Indian and take him with me as a slave," said Kinney.

"The first thing you know, that Indian will escape and tell the other Indians and they will kill all of us," the elder Bonney warned. Kinney retorted: "I generally have my way. Any man that crosses me, regrets it. I have had to kill two or three men already because they interfered with me. If you want any trouble you know how to get it."

Kinney rode his mule to the Indian, jumped off and struck the man over the head. The Indian fought back, but he was no match for the 225-pound Texan. Handcuffed, he was dragged to Kinney's hack and tied to it with a rope around his neck. His captor slashed him across the back with a blacksnake whip and told his wife to drive on. The Indian threw himself on the ground, where he was dragged by the neck. Kinney kept whipping him until he got up and trotted along behind the hack.

For several days Kinney rode behind the Indian, slashing him with the blacksnake to "break his spirit." Finally he untied him and told his ox driver to teach him how to drive the team. Then, after two or three weeks, Kinney stopped tying the Indian at night. The Texan had a hound

The mighty Snake River is calm in passing the site of Fort Hall.

dog he had used to trail runaway slaves. If the Indian ran away, he said, he would follow him and kill him to show other Indians how superior the white man was.

One dark windy night the Indian disappeared without a sound. When Kinney woke up, he found that his captive had taken a blanket, three hams, a powder horn, some lead and a favorite Kentucky rifle that had cost $100. Kinney was in a terrible rage. Although everyone in the train rejoiced over the Indian's escape, it seemed wiser to sympathize with the furious man.

Fort Hall became a registered national historic landmark in 1962.

Kinney saddled his mule, called his dog and set out to track his victim. But the wind had blown the sand into ridges, completely erasing the trail. After hunting for half a day in all directions, Kinney had to return to camp.

There is no other record to support this account, but Kinney does not seem to have made warm friends in the far west. He returned to the States after less than a year in California.

By September 12, after five weeks on the trail, Snyder wrote in his diary, "Our provisions are nearly gone." The last bag of flour had been opened, and only five pounds of bacon and eight pounds of dried buffalo meat remained. There was plenty of coffee, however. The train covered 25 miles of desert that day and sometimes there was not a spear of grass or any other vegetation for miles at a stretch.

The next day the company reached the Humboldt Sink after another 25-mile journey. The Truckee River, with pure water and abundant grass, was 40 miles ahead. But the last leg of the desert journey was one of the worst because the day was "oppressively hot," with no shade and no water along the way. The temperature was probably well over 100°. The mounted men reached the river at 11 p.m. and the wagons rolled in the next morning at 7. "The change from a barren waste to a wooded country was one of the most pleasant I have enjoyed for years," Snyder wrote.

The company rested two days while the animals grazed and drank, and then started up the river. The Greenwoods again chose the route through Dog Valley to avoid the difficult ascent of the upper Truckee.

Ten men, including Snyder, pushed ahead on horseback. On September 21 the advance party passed Donner Lake and saw the cabin where young Moses Schallenberger had spent the winter. The climb to the summit of Donner Pass was so hard the horses had to be led. Crossing the ridge, the party descended to Summit Valley and encamped on the headwaters of the Yuba River. A party of hunters fired several shots at deer but returned without any game.

The thick underbrush had to be cut down in many places before the horses could pass, but the men reached Bear River on September 23. Here they examined a cabin where the women of the 1844 train had been sheltered while waiting for help from Sutter's Fort. Some of the trees had been cut off eight feet above ground, indicating the depth of the snow.

Visiting Indians leave a 1967 festival at Fort Hall reservation.

Three days later Snyder wrote, "Men in bad humor. Expected to reach the plains ere this." Happily, at 1 p.m. the company at last got a view of the Sacramento Valley. But the arrival at Sutter's Fort was delayed a full day when faces and hands broke out with bad attacks of ivy poisoning. Snyder said his face "swelled so bad that I could not see."

On September 29 the men mounted their horses at 2:30 a.m. to avoid the scorching heat of the valley. They reached

79

Sutter's at noon, and Snyder's only comment on New Helvetia, as the Swiss emigrant had named his domain, was that he found "provisions of every kind scarce and high."

In October the wagons began to roll in to the fort. The emigrants told how the ascent of Donner Pass had tested the strength of both animals and men. One family spent three days climbing the six miles from Donner Lake to the summit. Nor was it easy to make the descent. Small trees were cut down and lashed to the hind end of each wagon to slow it down and keep it from turning over. Sarah E. Healy, who was an 18-year-old girl when she crossed the mountains on horseback, recalled years later that her saddle had slipped over the horse's head as she went down a steep slope. The considerate pony stopped.

The worries of the emigrants were as bad as their hardships. An eastbound pack train had alarming news: The Mexicans would take all of the North Americans prisoners as soon as they reached California. "Some of our company wanted to stop and build a fort, and spend the winter there," Mrs. Healy said, "but on further consideration it was thought better to risk the Spaniards, than to be shut up in the midst of these high mountains to starve. So we hastened on our way, losing no time to meet our fate, be it what it might."

One night, during the crossing of the Sierra Nevada, the party was awakened by a terrific explosion that shook the ground. A keg of powder on one of the wagons had somehow been ignited and had blown the wagon to pieces. Luckily, no lives were lost, but the explosion stirred suspicion. The owner of the wagon, Thomas Knight, had gone ahead to Sutter's Fort in order to hire pack mules to lighten his load, for his teams were weak. Captain Sutter's price was more than Knight could pay, so he returned to the train and learned of the explosion that had blasted the strongbox in which he carried his money. Although $18 was found

80

on the ground, several hundred dollars in gold and silver were missing. Apparently the powder had been fired by someone who knew about the money and wanted to conceal the theft. Knight finally got a confession from the guilty man, "but that did not help me," he wrote.

The wagons piloted by Old Greenwood began straggling into New Helvetia on October 16, when five arrived close to midnight. More came on October 18, 19, 20, 21, 24 and 25. And on October 30 the daily log carried this brief entry: "Mr. Greenwood and sons arrd from Feather River."

The entry said "and sons," which indicates that John Greenwood had not been banished after killing the Indian. Young Benjamin F. Bonney, less than seven years old, may have erred in his recollection long afterward—or Old Greenwood may have cooled off.

What we do know is that Caleb helped bring about 50 wagons into California in 1845; another 10 may have followed his parties. Between 250 and 300 emigrants had crossed the Sierra before the heavy snows closed the pass, and their wagons had traveled all the way from the Missouri River. California was being joined to the Union—just as the Mexicans feared.

Alexander L. Crosby

A typical scene on the Forty-Mile Desert.

10
Change of Flags

JOHN AUGUSTUS SUTTER WAS WORRIED as 1845 drew to a close. He had a vast domain of fertile land in the Sacramento Valley—some 98,000 acres, about the size of Brooklyn, New York. It was a gift from the Mexican government, of which he had become a citizen. The government asked only that he fortify his holdings and build a strong Mexican outpost.

Sutter had done so. But he had no intention of just sitting by the Sacramento River and counting his cows. He wanted to attract settlers by selling them land and supplies. What worried Sutter was that a good many of the emigrants whom Old Greenwood had brought across the Sierra were settling farther west around Sonoma, in the Napa Valley. The Mexican government did not want the North Americans there and was threatening to stop the emigration. Sutter wanted the emigration to continue, with the emigrants buying his land.

Caleb Greenwood and his two sons were apparently among those who went over to the beautiful Napa Valley. One of the Greenwood boys — most likely John — is mentioned in the diary of James Clyman, who had taken the Overland Trail to Oregon and then moved to California in 1845. Writing in March 1846 from the head of the Napa Valley, he said: "a young Mr. Greenwood came in having been out some weeks hunting and Trapping in the mountains north (around Clear Lake) he brought in a beautifull specimin of pure Sulpher and he informs me he saw greate Quantities of this mineral as Likewise a mineral resembling galena Lead ore in great abundance—but as Mr. Greenwood had the ill luck to loose his specimens (of) Lead ore I cannot say what kind of mineral it was."

A little over a month later, Clyman was starting back to the east with a small party. Old Greenwood and his two sons were part of the company, but we do not know how far east they went. Although Clyman's diary is one of the best ever kept by a western pioneer, the author paid more attention to scenery than to people.

The company assembled in Bear Valley. Clyman was impatient to start, so they began to climb the Sierra on April 29, although Old Greenwood had undoubtedly warned they would soon be in deep snow. The travelers had a miserable time, for there was no way to dodge the white blanket, up to eight feet deep. Softened by spring air, the crust would not support the pack horses, which sank to their bellies and then floundered. But on the third day the pack train reached the summit where the snow was solid enough for easy travel. The descent to Donner Lake was tough; the horses had to be unpacked, forced over ledges and then repacked. It took three hours to travel one mile, and there was a general sigh of relief when bare ground was seen at the lake. But it was not until the next day that grass was found for the half-starved animals, which had gone without food for three days.

Clyman noticed that the nearly naked Washoe Indians along the Truckee River did not complain of cold, "allthough we can hardly get clothes enough on us to keep ourselves comfortable." The wind from the southwest was "so strong that it nearly blew some of the Ladies from their saddles and we could see that the mountains behind us experienced an awfull snow storm."

East of present Reno, the party came upon a floating fishing machine, or raft, from which fish were speared. An old Indian hid when the whites arrived, but he was persuaded to come out. He slept with the company that night and made a gift of several large salmon trout in the morning.

Striking out across the desert, the company reached Brady's Hot Springs. Here there was a sad accident, as reported by Clyman: "Into one of these muddy pools my little water spaniel Lucky went poor fellow not knowing that it was Boiling hot. He deliberately walked in to the caldron to slake his thirst and cool his limbs when to his sad disappointment and my sorrow he scalded himself allmost instantly to death. I felt more for his loss than for any other animal I ever lost in my life as he had been my constant companion in all my wanderings since I Left Milwaukee."

Clyman had a sharp eye for geology. He commented that the mountains bordering the Humboldt River Valley were all of vitrified rock of various hues, mostly dark and brown. The floor of the valley was of hard, whitish mud, with no vegetation except a thorny shrub called grease wood which seemed to thrive without moisture.

As the party neared present Winnemucca, Clyman counted the noses of people and animals. The company included 19 men and boys, 3 women, 2 children and about 150 horses and mules. There were too many animals, he wrote, because in early May the grass was too young and short for good grazing. This entry was for May 13. Clyman did not learn until many weeks later that the United States had declared war on Mexico that day.

Three days later the party divided so the grass would have a little time to grow between grazings. Clyman and 8 other persons moved ahead, taking 37 animals. The pilot of this group was Lansford W. Hastings, an Ohio lawyer

Charles Kelly

Above: Brady's Hot Springs, where Clyman's dog jumped in and died.

Alexander L. Crosby

Below: Bypassed by Interstate 80, Brady's has declined in recent years.

whose secret ambition was to be president of a Republic of California. He was interested in a shorter route for emigrants and had been told by Fremont that many miles could be saved by crossing the Great Salt Lake Desert instead of following Snake River, 150 miles north.

When Clyman and Hastings reached the western edge of the desert, the absolutely bare wasteland extended eastward as far as they could see. After serious debate, they gambled on the unknown. Luckily the weather was cool, and the party crossed the 80-mile waterless stretch in 20 hours of riding. Clyman called the desert the most desolate spot on the whole globe. This route, which joined the Overland Trail at Fort Bridger, became known later as the Hastings Cutoff.

The Greenwoods stayed with the rest of the party and took the familiar trail north to Snake River and Fort Hall. They probably reached the fort about June 7.

Where Old Greenwood went next is uncertain. He may have gone through South Pass to the Sweetwater River and met his younger children, perhaps at the famous landmark, Independence Rock. Since neither Caleb nor his children could read or write, it would have been difficult to arrange a rendezvous. Still, the mountain men had a wonderful talent for getting messages to remote places, as was shown by the successful rendezvous of the fur traders. Thousands of trappers and Indians would come to the appointed place on the appointed day, despite the lack of telephones, mail service and literacy.

In any case, there is a definite record of the younger Greenwoods in California after the summer of 1846. And it seems almost certain that the old pathfinder would have been their pilot.

There is no doubt at all about the return of John Greenwood to California. On October 30, in Sonoma, Captain John Grigsby was signing up recruits for the war against

Pilot Peak, landmark on the west edge of the Great Salt Desert.

Mexico. Grigsby had been captain of the emigrant company that Old Greenwood had brought from Fort Hall in 1845, and it was on that journey that John had killed an Indian. One of the recruits was "Jno. Greenwood," who served as a private until April 10, 1847, earning $25 a month plus $4 for subsistence. When he collected his pay of $133.39 upon discharge, he signed the voucher with an X. Like his father, John had never learned to read or write.

The important battles of the Mexican War were fought on what is still Mexican territory, but there were skirmishes and maneuvers in California. The North Americans started the campaign by seizing the presidio at Sonoma before they knew the United States had declared war. Not a shot was fired as the Mexican flag was hauled down and the Bear Flag of California went up.

Commodore John D. Sloat officially raised the United States flag at Monterey in July. Captain Fremont's men skirmished with the native troops in the Salinas Valley and

87

were getting the worst of it until Colonel Stephen W. Kearny arrived from Santa Fe with a small force. Kearny's soldiers were combined with the sailors of Commodore Robert F. Stockton and the North American volunteers, making an army of 600 which fought the Mexicans at San Gabriel and La Mesa in January. Defeated, the Mexicans yielded the rich state to their mighty neighbor.

The change of flags did not bring prosperity to John Sutter at New Helvetia. When gold was discovered on his land in 1848, the frantic mob of gold-seekers swarmed over his property, killing cattle, digging everywhere. Sutter appealed to the United States government for compensation. The federal courts ruled that he did not have a sound title to his lands, and in 1880 the famous Swiss died in Washington—a bankrupt. Congress had adjourned on the day of his death without acting on his claim for damages.

Caleb Greenwood took no part in the Mexican War. The 83-year-old mountain man was in the mountains north of San Francisco Bay, hunting and fishing and having a wonderful time.

11
What He Looked Like

Old Greenwood was never photographed. But he comes to life in a description written by Edwin Bryant, a Kentucky emigrant of 1846. It is a splendid portrait at a mountain camp, well adorned with mountain language. Caleb was then 83 years old.

Bryant was at Sutter's Fort when a courier brought word that the war against Mexico had spread to California. The Kentuckian set out October 30, 1846, with a man named A. J. Grayson to recruit emigrants and Indians to help Captain Fremont defend Monterey, about 140 miles to the south. Their first destination was Sonoma, some 60 miles southwest of Sutter's Fort. They swam their horses across the Sacramento River and kept themselves dry in a canoe. Overtaking a company of emigrants bound for the Napa Valley, they camped with them overnight and signed up five men as volunteers.

A chilly rain fell most of the second day. The two recruiters were glad to find a dry roof that night at a cabin on Cache Creek where Mrs. Grayson was staying. Next morning the sun shone warmly. Bryant and Grayson rode to the top of the range bordering Cache Creek and paused for a breathtaking view of the Sacramento plain and the surrounding mountains. They crossed a broad plateau, dropped into a grassy valley and climbed another high ridge. From this they descended through a crevice in a precipice,

89

just wide enough for their horses. Often the animals had to slide down nearly perpendicular rocks.

The horsemen expected to sleep that night in Elias Barnett's house, which was somewhere in the picturesque valley they had entered. Hopefully they followed cattle trails again and again, but none of the trails led anywhere. So, at 10 p.m., they camped under a live oak tree and built a blazing fire to warm themselves after a ride of 40 miles.

The next morning they found Barnett's house a few miles up the valley but it was empty. Although corn and wheat had been harvested that year, there was no sign of the grain or the owner.

Nudging their horses up another mountain, the men were drenched with a cold rain at the cloud-covered summit. After three or four miles along high ground, they rode down into a romantic valley dotted with low conical hills. Here they met four Indians who wore dressed skins and carried long bows. Bryant and Grayson tried to find out where the Indians came from and where they were going, but sign language was a failure.

A few miles farther, five old and thin Indian women were seen, gathering grass seed for bread. Using a woven basket shaped like a shield, each woman would brush the heads of the stalks, throwing the seeds into a deep basket held in the other hand. The travelers could not get answers to their questions. The women simply pointed across a stream toward the *rancheria.*

Fording the little river, Bryant and Grayson struck a trail which led to the *rancheria,* two miles away. A dozen naked men, women and children appeared. The chief speaker indicated by signs that the overseer was away and would not return until several suns had risen and set. The travelers made signs of hunger. The Indians brought a loaf made of ground acorns mixed with a wild fruit, and they also brought water in a tightly woven basket.

90

Bryant was worried. He knew that he and Grayson had traveled off their course. Clouds hid the sun, and he had no compass. It was already 3 p.m. Could the Indian spokesman lead them to Sonoma? The man pointed in a direction that seemed wrong. But he insisted Sonoma was that way, and he finally agreed to guide them in exchange for Bryant's shirt.

The three took off. Soon they were deluged with cold rain. Bryant persuaded the Indian to stay with them by lending him his overcoat. After crossing several rocky hills, they reached a large timbered valley just before sunset. A sheet of water extended into the misty distance.

The Indian was delighted to see the water, and Bryant concluded they were actually looking at San Francisco Bay. Descending into the valley, they followed a small stream for two or three miles. At twilight they heard the tinkling of a cowbell across the stream. Bryant roared a halloo, and in a moment there came an answering halloo.

"Who the devil are you—Spaniards or Americans?" the unseen person shouted.

"Americans."

"Show yourself, then, damn you, and let us see the color of your hide."

"Tell us where we can cross the stream and you shall soon see us."

"Ride back and follow the sound of my voice, and be damned to you, and you can cross the stream with a deer's jump."

Guided by a string of shouts in the gathering dark, the horsemen found the crossing and were greeted by three hunters. Their leader was Old Greenwood himself. He invited them to his camp nearby, where a huge log fire was burning.

Bryant soon learned that his Indian guide had led him in the wrong direction. The body of water was not San

High hills near Clear Lake, where Old Greenwood went hunting.

Francisco Bay but Clear Lake, about 60 miles north of the bay. This disappointment was almost forgot when the half-starved visitors saw so much bear meat and venison that the camp looked like a butcher shop. Enjoying the hospitality of the mountains, the travelers ate boiled grizzly bear and roasted venison until they could eat no more. There was no bread. The mountain men generally did without it.

Let Bryant tell the rest of the story from his book, *What I Saw in California,* published in 1848:

> The hunting party consisted of Mr. Greenwood, Mr. Turner, Mr. Adams, and three sons of Mr. G., one grown, and the other two boys 10 or 12 years of age, half-breed Indians, the mother being a Crow. One of these boys is named "Governor Boggs" after ex-governor Boggs of

Missouri, an old friend of the father. Mr. Greenwood, or "Old Greenwood," as he is familiarly called, according to his own statement is 83 years of age, and has been a mountain trapper between 40 and 50 years. He lived among the Crow Indians, where he married his wife, between thirty and forty years. He is about six feet in height, raw-boned and spare in flesh, but muscular, and notwithstanding his old age, walks with the erectness and elasticity of youth. His dress was of tanned buckskin, and from its appearance one would suppose its antiquity to be nearly equal to the age of its wearer. It had probably never been off his body since he first put it on.

"I am," said he, "an old man—eighty-three years—it is a long time to live; —eighty-three years last ——. I have seen all the Injun varmints of the Rocky Mountains, —have fout them—lived with them. I have many children—I don't know how many, they are scattered; but my wife was a Crow. The Crows are a brave nation, —the bravest of all the Injuns; they fight like the white man; they don't kill you in the dark like the Black-foot varmint, and then take your scalp and run, the cowardly reptiles. Eighty-three years last ——; and yet old Greenwood could handle the rifle as well as the best on 'em, but for this infernal humor in my eyes, caught three (two) years ago in bringing the emigrators over the de-sart." (A circle of scarlet surrounded his weeping eyeballs.)

"I can't see jist now as well as I did fifty years ago, but I can always bring the game or the slinking and skulking Injun. I have jist come over the mountains from Sweetwater with the emigrators as pilot, living upon bacon, bread, milk, and sich like mushy stuff. It don't agree with me; it never will agree with a man of my age, eighty-three last ——; that is a long time to live. I thought I would take a small hunt to get a little exercise for my old bones, and some good fresh meat. The grisly bear, fat deer, and poultry, and fish—them are such things as a man should eat. I came up here where I knew there was plenty.

"I was here twenty years ago, before any white man see this lake and the rich land about it. It's filled with big fish. Thar's beer-springs (soda springs) here, better than them in the Rocky Mountains; thar's a mountain of solid brimstone (sulphur), and thar's mines of gold and silver, all of which I know'd many years ago, and I can show them to you if you will go with me in the morning. These black-skinned Spaniards have rebel'd again. Wall, they can make a fuss, damn 'em, and have revolutions each year, but they can't fight. It's no use to go arter 'em, unless when you ketch 'em you kill 'em. They won't stand an' fight like men, an' when they can't fight longer give up; but the skared varmints run away and then make another fuss, damn 'em."

Old Greenwood's talk around the camp fire may not have been the whole truth. Had he really been in California 20 years before? There is no other report on such an early trip. Were there actually mines of gold and silver in the Clear Lake area? No one has seen them. Caleb was a mountain man, and the mountain men could spin a yarn as readily as they could skin a deer. But Caleb's talk rang true in his heartfelt admiration for his Indian wife and her people of the Crow nation.

Bryant was impressed by the terrific swearing of Greenwood's friend, Turner. "I had heard mountain swearing before, but his went far beyond all former examples," the Kentuckian wrote. "He could do all the swearing for our army in Mexico, and then have a surplus."

After a big breakfast the next morning, no doubt consisting of bear meat and venison, Bryant and Grayson started back on their trail, carrying a two-day supply of bear meat and venison. They left their Indian pilot at the *rancheria,* with Bryant's shirt as promised. Then, following directions given by Old Greenwood, they found a trail which led to the Napa River, only a dozen miles from Sonoma.

12
The Donner Tragedy

T HE GRASSY HILLS OF CALIFORNIA are as brown as straw
in the dry summer months, for they are indeed covered
with the stalks of dead grass—except for the dark green
of live oaks. In the Sierra, there are patches of color from
lupine, fireweed, lilies and other flowers, but soon the plants
shed their seeds and die.

The wet season in California is winter. When the rains
cover the coastal hills and central valleys with new grass,
snow buries the Sierra, often to a depth of 20 feet or more.

In 1846 the winter rains came in the first week of November. While Edwin Bryant and A. J. Grayson were being
drenched on their way to Sonoma, heavy snow was falling
in the mountains. The passes were soon closed. Trapped

95

on the eastern slope of the Sierra were the 87 men, women and children of the Donner party, who had been forced to make camp at what has long since been called Donner Lake.

The Donner party, led by George and Jacob Donner and James Frazier Reed, had left Illinois in April 1846. The route chosen was by way of Fort Bridger instead of by Greenwood's Cutoff to Fort Hall. Arriving at Bridger's post on July 27, the company rested four days and decided to save time by taking the new Hastings Cutoff across the Great Salt Lake Desert.

The decision was costly because much of the trail to the desert had to be cleared for wagons. (This became the wagon road of the Mormons the next summer.) Further, many oxen died on the 80-mile desert, and their wagons had to be abandoned. Supplies were becoming short, and so were tempers.

From the springs at the western edge of the desert, the party dispatched Charles T. Stanton and William Mc-Cutchen on horseback to seek supplies from Sutter. Then, as the emigrants moved down the Humboldt River, James Reed got into a violent argument with a teamster, and killed him in self-defense. Banished by his fellow travelers, Reed rode ahead, leaving his wife and four children.

Near Bear Valley, on the western slope of the Sierra, he met Stanton on his way back from Sutter's. Reed thought that Stanton was not carrying enough food so, when he reached Sutter's on October 28, he got additional supplies. McCutchen, exhausted by his trip, had been recovering at Sutter's. He was able to start back with Reed, but the two men were stopped by impassable snow when they were 30 miles from Donner Lake. They had to turn back to Sutter's.

John Sutter reassured them. He pointed out that by slaughtering their cattle and rationing their food, the Donners had a good chance of living through the winter. Hadn't

96

John A. Sutter chose a full dress uniform for this oil painting.

Moses Schallenberger survived the winter of 1844? Others in the same party had come through without loss of life. By February, Sutter said, the snow should be compact enough for travel and the worst storms might be over.

But Reed could not rest. Sutter then advised him to go

to Yerba Buena (not yet named San Francisco) and appeal to the naval authorities. There was a shortage of men around Sutter's because of enlistments in the war against Mexico.

Reed spent an agonizing two months getting to Yerba Buena, which was less than 100 miles from Sutter's Fort. Traveling by land around San Francisco Bay, he found at San Jose that the Mexicans were in control on the San Francisco side. Reed signed up with a company of volunteers. A skirmish at Santa Clara on January 2 ended the war in the north, but Reed was not released from military service until late in the month.

He hastened north to Yerba Buena and talked to Commodore J. B. Hull of the Navy, the acting governor. The officer was sympathetic, but doubted whether the Navy Department would approve the cost of a relief expedition to the Donner party. Reed then conferred with some leading citizens. The result was that Mayor Washington A. Bartlett, a lieutenant of the Navy, called a public meeting on February 3, at which $800 was contributed and committees were appointed to raise more. Commodore Hull chipped in $50. Since nearly everybody in San Francisco had come by sea, the concern for overland emigrants was heartening.

Preparations for the rescue moved rapidly. A launch was provided to carry an expedition up the Sacramento River. Midshipman Selim E. Woodworth was authorized to direct the party.

On February 5, when the launch was about to leave, Captain Sutter's launch, the *Sacramento,* arrived with a letter bearing dreadful news. Five women and two men from the Donner party, with bleeding bare feet, had reached Johnson's Ranch, north of Sutter's Fort. They had struggled through the snow for 32 days. They had eaten their moccasins, the strings of their snowshoes, and the bodies of seven men who had died of starvation and exhaustion. All of the women had survived.

Looking east to Donner Lake from the old highway in Donner Pass.

What had happened was that, after crossing the last desert, the weary Donner party had camped in the green meadows by the Truckee River for several days so the animals could regain their strength. The delay was fatal. Although it was early November, heavy snow began to fall. The company could not move ahead. Rough cabins were built, and the hut left by young Schallenberger was reoccupied. The starving cattle wandered off and were covered by deep drifts. When the meager stock of provisions was eaten, the emigrants ate bark, twigs, mice and, eventually, the bodies of those who died. Jacob Donner and three others had died by December 10.

Finally, on December 16, the 15 strongest persons—10 men and 5 women—had started out on foot to get help. They had reached the summit, but one man had died within a week. By Christmas they had not eaten for four days and were too weak to go farther. A wild snowstorm struck. The 14 crouched around their campfire for an entire week.

The Donner party's camp in November 1846, before the deep snow.

When the skies cleared, four men were dead, and cannibalism began.

Captain Sutter called for volunteers to carry food across the mountains to the Donner party. Fourteen men responded. Beef cattle were killed, and the meat dried over fires. Flour was ground. The skins of the animals were cut into strips for snowshoes, which were made by peeling a pine branch, heating it over a fire and bending it into a bow about two feet long and one foot wide. The leather strips made a lattice work.

After three days of preparations the First Donner Relief left Johnson's Ranch on February 5 with beef, bread and sugar. There was no guide. When the snow became eight feet deep, the mules could go no farther and six men quit. Leaving one man in charge of the mules, the other seven kept climbing. Each one carried about 75 pounds of meat.

from an old lithograph

Seven men of the First Donner Relief arrived in February 1847.

The snow got deeper and deeper. The men traveled Indian file, and at each step the leader sank to his knees. When he became too tired to keep lifting his snowshoes, he would fall to the rear and the next man would break the trail. A day's travel was four to six miles.

To mark their route and to make a signal for any emigrants who might be wandering in the mountains, the relief party set fire to every dead pine tree. Camp was made at night by felling a dozen young pines about six inches in diameter, cutting them to 12-foot lengths and laying them on the snow as a platform. A fire was built on top of the logs. After roasting some meat, the men pulled their blankets around their shoulders and dozed through the night.

Every now and then the rescuers got a glimpse of a lofty peak above Donner Lake. They had no guidance except this mountain.

101

At sunset on the sixteenth day the party crossed frozen Donner Lake and looked for the camp of the emigrants. Not a person, not a cabin, not a wisp of smoke, could be seen. The men raised a loud halloo. Presently a woman crawled out from a hole in the snow, and several other persons came from holes leading to their buried huts. Daniel Rhoads, one of the rescuers, recalled years later:

"They were gaunt with famine and I never can forget the horrible, ghastly sight they presented. The first woman spoke in a hollow voice very much agitated and said, 'Are you men from California or do you come from heaven?' "

The rescuers distributed their food sparingly, knowing that the penalty for over-eating would be death. The next morning they started their return trip with 21 emigrants, mostly women and children. The burned stumps of the pine trees guided them through the forest, but there was almost nothing to eat because martens had reached the food caches left in trees on the hike to Donner Lake.

The First Donner Relief party had crossed the summit and was approaching the mule camp when every heart was lifted by the sight of the Second Donner Relief, with Caleb Greenwood's son Britton as pilot.

At the mule camp that night the exhausted travelers ate dried beef and biscuits. The rest of the provisions had been hauled up into a pine tree. One 15-year-old boy, still famished, climbed the tree while the camp slept. He ate so much dried beef that he died the next day.

13

Caleb Joins the Rescue

CALEB GREENWOOD, CARRYING HIS 84 YEARS as lightly as his rifle, was one of the first to hear about the snowbound Donner party. He came into Yerba Buena from his camp in the Napa Valley, anxious to help rescue the emigrants. What he needed was men, money and supplies.

The citizens of Sonoma had pledged more than $500 if Greenwood could recruit enough men for the expedition. But to persuade a dozen experienced men to brave the deep snows of the Sierra, Greenwood knew he would need immediate cash for warm clothing and wages. He appealed to Commodore Hull. Impressed by the sincerity of the old mountain man, the Navy officer issued an order for $400 and directed that horses, saddles and bridles be supplied.

Greenwood was joined in Yerba Buena by James Frazier Reed, the exile from the Donner party who had worked desperately to organize a relief expedition. The two men left Yerba Buena by a sailing ship on February 7. They sailed north to San Pablo Bay and traveled 12 miles overland to Sonoma. Here they separated temporarily. Caleb went to his camp in the north to get his son Britton, his friend John Turner and their horses. Reed got more horses from the Navy.

Reunited, the Greenwood party pushed across swollen streams and muddy hills, obtaining more recruits at several points. On February 17 the men reached the Sacramento, where the water was high. They went up the river to the mouth of Feather River and did not find Midshipman Woodworth's launch, which had been delayed by head winds and a stop at Sutter's for supplies. What they did see was a herd of about 100 elk. Rifles were quickly raised and two of the elk dropped.

Reed and Greenwood were going to make skin boats of elk hide for the river crossing, but they found a launch which carried the baggage across. The horses swam.

The last stop before the mountains was Johnson's Ranch, 25 miles up the Sacramento, where the five women and two men had come from the Donner party. Reed got to the ranch ahead of his party and put Johnson's Indians to work night and day grinding flour in a coffee mill, while he dried beef. Early in the morning of February 23 the party took off, carrying about half a ton of food on 11 horses and mules. Old Greenwood and Reed had combined to organize the Second Donner Relief. William McCutchen, who had a wife and daughter trapped in the snow, was with them. The First Donner Relief had an 18-day start on the second expedition.

In two days the Greenwood party reached the lower part of Bear Valley—and snow. Caleb had thought it might be feasible to drive horses across the divide and then slaughter them for the emigrants. But after 200 yards in the snow, it was obvious that the horses could go no farther. The snow had not compacted enough to support their weight. So the packs were shifted from the backs of horses to the backs of 15 men, and as the expedition moved forward "the hilarity commenced as usual," Reed noted in his diary. The mountaineers might be facing a fatal rendezvous, but that was all the more reason for a good laugh.

Somebody had to take charge of the horses and the reserve stock of provisions. Old Greenwood was given the assignment. Perhaps Reed and the others knew better than he

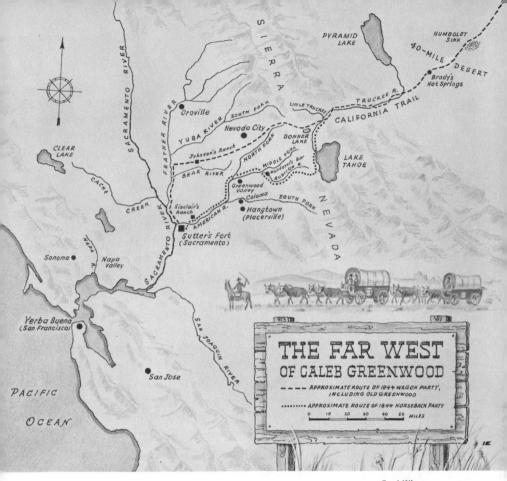

Fred Kliem

that there were limits to the strength of a man of 84. And they may have worried about his 9-year-old son, William Sublette Greenwood, who was with him. (Although the boy's name does not appear in any of the 1847 records, his wife wrote many years later that he had gone to the mountains with his father.) Britton Greenwood continued with the men on foot, acting as pilot.

On February 27, blessed with "a fine, hard snow," the Second Relief had traveled about four miles when there was a dramatic meeting in the forest. The seven men of the First

105

Relief were returning with 19 people who had been strong enough to walk from the Donner cabins (two had died along the way). But all of the rescued persons and their rescuers were in poor shape. Martens had eaten the food the First Relief had cached on its way to Donner Lake, and there had been little or no food during five days of exhausting travel up the mountain and over the summit.

Reed had been baking bread for two nights. As he passed the straggling line, handing out as much as he dared give, there was a constant cry of "Bread! Bread! Bread! Bread!" from adults as well as children. Reed's wife and two of his four children were in the group. "I cannot describe the death-like look they all had," Reed wrote in his diary.

There was no time to be lost, so after a few minutes the Second Relief pressed on. As the day warmed, the snow became too soft for walking and the party made camp. The approach of night brought freezing temperatures, enabling the rescuers to travel all night and through the next morning. At noon they reached the first camp, that of Patrick Breen and his family. The Breens were in pretty good shape, but some of their neighbors were very feeble. Leaving men to cook and care for the weak, Reed, McCutchen and two others continued to Alder Creek, where the Donners had camped.

George Donner was helpless. Reed urged his wife to leave, promising that one of his men would stay to care for him and for Mrs. Jacob Donner, whose husband had died in December. Mrs. Donner refused to go. Her children had been taken out, she said, and she would not leave her husband. "After repeatedly urging her to come out, I was satisfied in my own mind that Mrs. Geo. Donner remained with her husband from pure love and affection," Reed wrote later.

At noon the next day the Second Relief started back for Sutter's, taking all who were able to travel. Reed left as

106

much food as he could spare, counting on Midshipman Woodworth's Third Relief to bring more provisions in a few days.

On their way to the cabins, Reed's party had made three caches of dried beef. At two locations they had tied a bag to the top of a pine sapling, then cut off all the branches to protect the meat from animals. Reed now sent two experienced mountain men ahead to get the last cache and meet the party the next day.

Camp was made on 20 feet of snow, at a spot where the First Relief had camped and built a fire. During the night a heavy snowstorm began. It lasted through the next day and night and up until noon of the following day. All of the food was eaten. One child died.

The two mountaineers returned with bad news. Wolverines had destroyed the first cache of beef, so the men had trudged on to the second. It was partly gone. Then the storm had struck, and there was nothing to do except wait.

With clear skies, the party prepared to leave. But Patrick Breen refused to move. He said that if he had to die, he would rather die in camp than along the way. Reed and his companions remonstrated with him. They pointed out that his family was strong enough to travel and if the party must perish, let them all die together in an effort to get out. Breen would not budge. Losing patience, Reed asked some of his men to witness his declaration "that if his family died, their blood be upon his head, and not on ours." Seven others stayed with the Breens in what was called "Starved Camp."

The weather turned bitterly cold after the storm. When camp was made for the night of March 8, many of the party had frozen feet. Walking the next day was agony for those who had been frostbitten. But they trudged forward, slowly, and reached the camp prepared by the advance members of the group. The stragglers made so much noise that they aroused a nearby camp—the camp of Midshipman Wood-

Britton Greenwood at about 30 years.

worth, who had been proceeding to the rescue with great caution. He had a party of sailors with him. After brief contact with the snow of the Sierra, their preference for the sea was confirmed.

Woodworth sent a couple of sailors to invite the Second Relief to sleep at his encampment. Since most of the new arrivals were bedded down, they declined, but asked for something to eat. Food was then supplied.

In the morning Reed and his men urged Woodworth to go immediately to the relief of those still in the cabins, and of the Breen party at Starved Camp in Yuba Valley. The Breens had no food at all, and the provisions at the cabins were meager. But Woodworth said he could not proceed without a pilot. The mountaineers pointed out that no pilot would be needed to the Yuba Valley because he could follow the tracks left by their snowshoes. And the Yuba River was a sure guide to the lake near the cabins. Woodworth was unmoved by these arguments. He said he had to have a pilot.

After two days of debate, the naval officer finally agreed to pay $3 a day to any man who would go back to Donner Lake, with a bonus of $50 to anyone who brought out a child not his own. The Third Donner Relief party of seven men was then organized, including two men who had been in the Second Relief. Midshipman Woodworth remained in the Bear River Valley and never got anywhere near the summit of the Sierra.

The Third Donner Relief reached Starved Camp in two days and was shaken by a terrible sight. The campfire had melted the snow, making a pit 20 feet deep and some 15 feet across. At the bottom the seven Breens and four children of other families were still alive. They had been eating two children and one woman who had died.

The sky was darkening with the clouds of an approaching storm. But only two of the 11 souls were able to walk. What could be done? The relief party decided to take out the four children and leave the Breen family. After all, the Breens could have been saved by following James Reed.

But John Stark, one of the rescuers, disagreed. "No, gen-

109

A summer view of the site of the Donner camp, near Donner Lake.

tlemen, I will not abandon these people," he said. "I am here on a mission of mercy, and I will not half do the work. You can all go if you want to, but I shall stay by these people while they and I live."

Stark was a huge man, weighing 224 pounds — not the ideal type for snowshoeing. But he stuck with the Breen family, alone, and he saved their lives. As John Breen wrote later, "There was probably no other man in California at that time, who had the intelligence, determination, and the immense physical powers of John Stark. He was as strong as two ordinary men. On his broad shoulders, he carried the provisions, most of the blankets, and most of the time some of the weaker children. He would laughingly say that he could carry them all, if there was room on his back, because they were so light from starvation."

Stark was eventually paid $117 for 39 days of service, plus $50 for bringing out a 7-year-old boy. "No man in the history of the Donner Relief took a more honorable part," Dale Morgan wrote in *Overland in 1846*.

110

"Indomitable, unafraid," reads this tribute to the Donner party.

Continuing to the cabins on Donner Lake, the rest of the relief party found that six more persons had died and only nine were left. The rescuers returned to Johnson's Ranch with those who could travel and on March 23 another seven-man party tried to reach the cabins. This group gave up at Bear Valley on the western slope. Finally the huge mountain man, William O. Fallon, took a party to the lake in April and discovered only one man still alive.

Out of the 81 people who had been trapped by snow, only 45 reached the Sacramento Valley. The four Reed children were saved, but the McCutchens lost their daughter.

We do not know what happened to Caleb after he was left in charge of the horses of the Second Relief. But in 1906 Sarah Greenwood, who had married William Sublette Greenwood, wrote this:

There was a lady among them who had become insane. Her husband had died of starvation. She gave them a great deal of trouble, every time she got a chance she would slip off of her horse and try to get back to her husband but they managed to get to Emigrant Gap with her. There my husband's father Caleb Greenwood strapped her on a horse and my husband the 9-year-old boy led the horse by a halter into Sacramento (Sutter's Fort) and carried the little girl behind him. He never knew who the lady or little girl was. This is not second hand talk. I have it from my husband's own mouth.

Britton Greenwood, a youth of 20 or less, lost several of his toes from frostbite. The Greenwood men did all they could to save a party that was dogged by bad luck.

14

Stockton's Journey

IF CALEB GREENWOOD HAD EVER WANTED to have his own ranch in California and raise cows, chickens or cantaloupes, he would have gone back to the Napa Valley after the Donner Relief and stayed there. Old Greenwood wasn't that kind of man, which is why his story makes a book.

Not much is known about the Greenwood family for the two years after the Donner expedition. John Greenwood was discharged from the California Battalion on April 12, 1847, just about the time his father and two brothers reached Sutter's Fort from the mountains. Caleb's four-year-old daughter, Sarah Mojave Greenwood, and her sister, Angeline, were probably still in the United States with relatives or friends. That may explain why Caleb turned east again in 1847, taking his sons with him.

It was a rare mountain man who wanted any of his children to accompany him on his travels. Hardships were certain, and danger was always near. Caleb probably felt confident that he could watch out for his young until they learned to take care of themselves. And there is good reason to believe that he loved and needed the children of his devoted Crow wife, Batchicka, then dead four years.

Old Greenwood went back to the States as guide for the party of Commodore Robert F. Stockton, who had commanded the Pacific squadron in the Mexican War and captured Los Angeles and San Diego. A flattering biography of Stockton, published in 1856, when he was thinking of himself as a future President, tells what happened on the journey.

The 49 members of the party left on July 20, 1847. The men were described as a mixed lot of trappers, hunters and sailors from the States, Canada, Mexico, Ireland and elsewhere. "Many were of the most desperate and lawless character," wrote Stockton's biographer. To keep these desperadoes under control, Stockton announced at the start that anyone who refused to obey his orders, or showed cowardice in any encounter with Indians, would be shot.

The Indians took a lively interest in the expedition. When the moon rose over a camp by the Truckee River, a volley of arrows whistled into the tents. Stockton ordered his men to frighten away the attackers by firing over their heads. The Indians, evidently concluding that the whites were hopelessly bad shots, returned at breakfast time and loosed another flight of arrows. One struck the Commodore, passing through his rear deck. Breaking the arrow in half, the officer quickly pulled out the shaft. Then, having heard that arrows were often poisoned, "he sent for one of the old trappers, a man who had lived twenty years among the Indians and had a Crow squaw for his wife, and asked him if he supposed the arrow to be poisoned."

Clearly this was Old Greenwood, who probably could not resist the temptation to scare the man who had threatened death to anyone who disobeyed him. Looking the Commodore fiercely in the eye, he replied: "Yes! by God! and you have not half an hour to live!"

If the Commodore was frightened, he knew it was prudent to pretend otherwise. "You old liar!" he was said to have retorted. "Do you suppose you can frighten me? If you had said I might die within a few days or a week, I might have thought you believed what you said. Begone out of my sight, before I blow out your brains!"

114

Old Greenwood is reported to have disappeared "as fast as he could run," a statement that hardly fits his character. The Commodore determined to have revenge on the Indians for their assault on his person. Held in camp an extra day by the illness of one of his men, he planned an ambush at a ford a half-mile away. By the time the moon rose, riflemen were hidden in the bushes at the edge of the river, with orders not to fire until the Indians were fording the stream. Presently a file of about fifty Indians began to move through the Truckee. Twenty rifles fired, almost simultaneously, and the Indians fled. There was no count of casualties; those killed or mortally wounded were swept away by the river. Stockton resumed his journey the next day, secure but not altogether comfortable in the saddle.

Never having seen a buffalo, the Commodore was anxious to meet the great beasts of the plains and test his skill as a hunter. One morning the party awoke and saw "the whole surface of the earth—to the distant horizon—covered with countless thousands of buffalo." The standard procedure was to ride to the leeward of the herd, dismount and crawl near enough for a sure shot. The Commodore declared this was not sporting. He ordered his companions to tighten their saddle girths and then charge on horseback. He promised he would bag two cows and would expect each hunter to get at least one. Digging in with his spurs, the Commodore galloped his horse toward the buffalo.

The Commodore's worshipful biographer continues:

> The chase of the buffalo pursued in this way is, perhaps, the most exciting and dangerous of all field-sports, not, perhaps, excepting that of lions and tigers in India and Africa. The horse rushes into the drove, and soon partakes of the alarm and terror with which he inspires the buffalo. A cloud of dust arises, obscuring all objects except those close at hand. The buffalo bulls roar; the earth trembles sensibly beneath the hoofs of the multitudinous animals as they rush

115

headlong onwards. The rider's whole strength is required to hold and guide his horse and keep the saddle—standing erect in his stirrups—the horse springing from one side to the other to avoid contact with the buffalo, and, snorting and plunging, requires a skilful and powerful hand to direct him.

Thus, bounding on, the hunter singles out the animal he prefers, and rides with it side-by-side till a favorable opportunity occurs for a successful shot. As soon as this is had, his next effort is to extricate himself from the herd. This he does by gradually dropping in the rear, and, when a favorable opening is observed through the drove to the right or left, guiding his horse out of the line of direction in which the buffalo are traveling. But, should the hunter unfortunately be thrown from his horse, the danger is imminent that the buffalo will trample him down.

The Commodore's horse had too much respect for naval authority to throw his rider. As every reader will guess, Stockton soon bagged his two cows, using his pistols. Then he gracefully withdrew from the herd, rode to the top of a hill and blew his horn. Finally the other hunters joined him. Each man said he had shot a buffalo, but the only ones found were those killed by the Commodore.

Pleased by his success, Stockton never missed a chance to kill a buffalo as the party moved across the plains. Buffalo meat was eaten three times a day and sometimes between meals. Altogether the Commodore was said to have killed 45 animals. Once he was confronted by a wounded bull that was about to charge. Although hunters had told him that a pistol bullet would not penetrate the thick skull, Stockton fired as his terrified horse sprang forward. Reining in his mount, he felt something wet on his face. It was blood. Then he noticed more blood on one ear of the horse. The bullet had gone through the ear and the frightened animal, shaking its head, had tossed blood into its rider's face. Needless to say, the buffalo was dead.

116

Uncontrolled shooting of buffalo almost wiped out the species.

At least one man in the party had cause to be thankful for the Commodore's passion for shooting buffalo. He was Peter Lassen, who got lost on the South Platte River. Luckily, he had four buffalo tongues with him, and he made them last 13 days. Lassen reached the Missouri frontier before Stockton, and lived to have a volcano named for him.

The Commodore's party arrived in St. Joseph at the end of October and disbanded. The biography solemnly reported: "Tears coursed down the weather-worn cheeks of the bold and hardy mountaineers, when they took the last friendly grip of the Commodore's hand. . . . Lawless, reckless, desperate, wicked, and callous, as many of them were, Stockton had found the tender spot in each man's heart and made a lodgment there."

It may be doubted whether Old Greenwood wept at the parting, but he probably refrained from giving the Commodore a friendly whack on his arrow-pierced thigh.

Commodore Robert F. Stockton.

The book, *A Sketch of the Life of Com. Robert F. Stockton,* did not develop enough steam to propel its subject into the White House. The Commodore lived profitably, however, as president of the Delaware and Raritan Canal Company, which transported barges between New Brunswick and Bordentown, New Jersey, until the railroads put the canal out of business. Long before then, the Commodore had gone to his happy hunting ground.

15
Last Trip West

OLD GREENWOOD'S RETURN TO CALIFORNIA is reported in a narrative written years later by Rufus G. Burrows, who was 14 when he went to California with his family in 1848. The boy's mother was in poor health. His stepfather, Rufus Hitchcock, had run a trading post in the fur country, where the trappers gave glowing reports of California and the Pacific Coast. Hoping that his wife's health would im-improve in the Sacramento Valley, he decided to take the family west.

The first stage of the journey was from the Hitchcock home near Kansas City to Fort Laramie, Wyoming, on the North Platte River. There a train of 51 wagons with about 200 persons was organized. A capable man named M. M. Wambough, who had traveled east with the Stockton party, was elected captain. The company had 250 oxen to haul the wagons, 50 saddle horses and between 200 and 300 head of cattle.

Prominent among the travelers were Old Greenwood, then 86, who was described as "a noted Indian fighter, trapper, hunter, etc.," and his four sons and two daughters. Burrows identified the sons as John, Billy, Boggs and Britt; he did not mention James, and it is possible that John was named in error for him. The names of the two girls were not given. (One was Sarah Mojave, who was then five, and the other was Angeline, who died after reaching California.)

119

"Old Bedlam," the officers' quarters at Fort Laramie, Wyoming.

So, at last, Caleb had brought all but one of his family together. There is no record of where the girls had lived since the death of their mother, or how Old Greenwood was able to find them. Sarah Mojave was only a baby when her father had gone west, and Angeline was probably too young to remember him. If Old Greenwood had not visited them before the reunion in 1848, the two little girls must have been astonished to learn that this towering, white-haired man in buckskins was their father.

The wagon train was delayed in the Sioux country by the illness of one emigrant. To get better feed for their stock, the Greenwoods and a young man named P. B. Cornwall went on ahead with a wagon. They were intercepted by some 500 Pawnee warriors who were trespassing on Sioux lands in pursuit of buffalo. The warriors helped themselves to everything in the wagon and, as they left, they shot five arrows toward Cornwall, just to scare him. The young man picked them up.

The Sioux were then at peace with the whites. Greenwood knew there was a Sioux village a short distance ahead, and he drove to it. Cornwall took his five arrows to the old chief.

"Pawnee, Pawnee, Pawnee!" the chief exclaimed, recognizing the arrows. "When the sun goes down, we will give them their arrows back with some of our own." Then the chief gave a loud yell, summoning his warriors. They came running from all over the village. The chief showed them the arrows and told them what they would do. The warriors went back to their tents.

Just before sundown, the warriors returned in war paint and feathers, mounted on their ponies. Led by the chief, they set out to find the Pawnee camp, which was discovered at quite a distance from the Sioux village. The warriors surrounded the camp and then waited until daybreak before attacking. The battle was fierce and deadly. About 50 Pawnees were killed—a terrible penalty for the prank in shooting five arrows at Cornwall. The rest of the band fled, leaving a large number of ponies and a quantity of dried buffalo meat.

The defeated warriors encountered Wambough's wagon train and were in a mood to attack. The captain instantly ordered the wagons corralled. "We are ready. Come on," he told an Indian boy who had been to a school in the east. The young warriors wanted to take up the challenge, but the older Pawnees knew their arrows were no match for the guns of the whites. Finally at sundown the Indians left, and the train hurried on to the Sioux village.

Along the Humboldt River one of the company was accidentally killed with a shotgun. To conceal his grave so the body would not be dug up and stripped by Indians, Wambough had the entire wagon train drive over the spot several times.

Fourteen-year-old Rufus, like Commodore Stockton, was

bent on hunting buffalo, and he had an Indian pony that had been trained for the chase. He started out one day with five men after a distant herd had been spotted through field glasses. One of the hunters made a successful shot, but Rufus's old flintlock gun would not fire. The boy turned back to camp and suddenly came upon three old bulls. The pony, knowing what to do, ran directly toward them. Rufus, knowing his gun wouldn't shoot, pulled frantically on the reins. One of the bulls wheeled to face the horse and rider, his hair standing on end (as Rufus's probably was, too).

"I at last got my pony to stop and turned him for camp," Rufus wrote. Then he added something that Commodore Stockton would never have said: "I had all the buffalo chasing that day I wanted."

While crossing the Forty-Mile Desert between the Humboldt Sink and the Truckee River, the party met a group of Mormons returning to Salt Lake. The Mormons had exciting news: Gold had been discovered by James Marshall at Coloma on the American River, where he was building a millrace for John A. Sutter. Marshall had found the nuggets in January; Wambough's train got the word in the middle of August.

When the company reached the cabins built by the Donner party, bones and skeletons were still lying on the ground. A day's halt was called so the men could gather up the last remains and bury them. Young Rufus noticed that the branches of the pines had been cut off far above ground by men gathering firewood while standing on the deep snow.

After the encounter with the Mormons, everyone in the train kept talking and thinking about gold. If the nuggets were lying in the beds of streams, anybody could pick them up and make a fortune. Old Greenwood and his sons were probably dreaming golden dreams as they hurried over the Sierra to the country they knew so well.

16
Gold and Blood

NEWS FROM CALIFORNIA in 1848 traveled not much faster than an active terrapin. Letters were carried around Cape Horn by sailing vessels, or across country by stagecoaches and wagon trains. Often months passed between posting and delivery. Not until 1860 would the pony express give 8-day service between Sacramento and the end of the telegraph line and railroad at St. Joseph. Not until October 1861 would the telegraph wires be carried across the Sierra.

The news of James Marshall's discovery in January 1848 at Coloma, 40 miles northeast of Sacramento, spread slowly in California. At first there was skepticism and little interest. But by spring Californians were flocking to the American River, and by summer every square foot of land had been claimed. Marshall's own claims were stolen. In later years Marshall said his gold discovery brought him little fame and less reward.

Reports of rich strikes were published in eastern newspapers in the early fall. In December 1848 an official announcement was made by President Polk in his message to Congress, touching off the great gold rush of 1849.

Old Greenwood and his sons went to Coloma soon after crossing the Sierra with the Wambough train. The little girls were left temporarily with some Spanish ladies, probably in the Napa Valley.

123

Coloma was a bustling, roistering village of about 40 log cabins and tents in the level valley by the South Fork of the American River. Dust was being churned up every minute by horses, wagon wheels and people. The steep slopes of the valley were studded with live oaks, pines and patches of manzanita.

In addition to gold-seekers, merchants, laborers, gamblers and adventurers of all sorts, the gold country was attracting writers and artists. Millions of readers in the United States and abroad wanted to know about life in the mining camps. Articles, letters, short stories and books were being produced at a fast pace, sometimes earning more for their authors and illustrators than could have been panned from the streams.

Fortunately, more than one writer turned a keen eye upon the Greenwoods. The family could hardly have been missed. Thus, Theodore T. Johnson wrote in his *Sights in the Gold Regions and Scenes by the Way*, published in 1849, "Among the most conspicuous characters in the valley were Old Greenwood and his sons. The former is a famous backwoodsman and trapper in the Rocky Mountains, who has pioneered many a party of emigrants to the head waters flowing to the Pacific."

The Greenwoods built themselves a one-room log cabin with vertical slabs, probably sawed from pine logs at James Marshall's mill. The cabin, about 10 by 15 feet, had a dirt floor. Furniture was meager, no more than a bench, a rough table, and some bunks. The walls had a few shelves for pots, dishes and supplies, and some pegs for clothing.

Johnson and his fellow traveler, S. S. Osgood, pitched their tent under an oak tree, close to the millrace where gold had been discovered. The two New Yorkers had sailed to the isthmus of Panama, crossed it and continued to San Francisco on a ship that arrived April 1, 1849. Eleven days later they reached Coloma, and one of their first actions

124

Above: Sutter's Mill, with dirt filling the tailrace, long after the gold discovery. The man in front has been said to be James Marshall.

Below: The modern reproduction of the mill stands back from the river.

was to sell as much of their burdensome equipment as they could.

Their tent was near the Greenwood cabin. Hearing the sound of a violin, the two men walked over and looked in. John Greenwood was seated on a saddle in one corner of the room, "fiddling away in first-rate style for two or three of his friends." A rifle stood in one corner. The shelves were well stocked with bottles of liquor and a great variety of cups. Old Greenwood did not depend on the American River to slake his thirst.

Although he had caught the gold fever, there is no evidence that Caleb consistently panned or dug for the precious metal. The reports from Coloma mention only his children as gold-seekers, and their methods were those of resourceful children. When a pony named Miss Jenny Lind, owned by Johnson and Osgood, disappeared, young Boggs Greenwood offered to find her for half an ounce of gold dust ($8) payable in advance. The New Yorkers rejected this deal and were lucky enough to recover their pony the next day with the help of an Indian vaquero.

Greenwood's youngest boys used to scrape up the dust around store counters and saloons. They would blow it and wash it, always finding a few particles of gold. Tying the treasure into corners of a handkerchief, they would peddle their daily hoard to earn $1 or more.

Sarah Mojave Greenwood and her sister Angeline were soon brought to the cabin at Coloma. Many years later Sarah remembered exchanging small bottles of gold dust for flour and sugar. She also recalled the time when she found an old rifle which had been bent and sawed off. It was a great prize for the children, who used it while playing Indians. The trigger would be squeezed, the hammer would click, and the intended victim would be assured that he was utterly dead.

Unknown to the children, the gun still held an old charge

126

which had never been exploded in their games. One day Sarah aimed at her father and pulled the trigger. This time the charge was fired, but its force was dissipated by age and by the bend in the barrel. Still, Caleb was slightly wounded. "My God! What have you done?" the old mountaineer exclaimed, jumping to his feet. Sarah never forgot the occasion, although we have no reason to think that Old Greenwood reinforced her memory with a willow switch.

The Digger Indians of the gold country were alarmed, understandably, when thousands of whites poured in. For as long as their oldest men could remember the history of the tribe, this land belonged to them. The Spaniards had taken over the fertile valleys, it is true, but the hills and mountain streams were still the domain of the first inhabitants. Now the clear streams were being turned into muddy sewers by men seeking specks of gold that could not fill an empty stomach or warm a chilly back.

There was conflict in the air, and neither the Indians nor the whites knew how it had begun. Actually, the story went back to 1810, when two of John Jacob Astor's partners in the fur trade founded Astoria, Washington. There were rumors that Indians were planning to attack the undermanned trading post. Duncan McDougall, one of the partners, had a bright idea. He showed some Indian scouts a tightly corked bottle. Inside, he said, were the spirits of smallpox, and he would pull the cork unless the Indians kept the peace. Terrified, the Indians fled. They did not forget about the bottle, and the tale of the white man's evil magic spread throughout the northwest.

A generation later, in 1847, there was an outbreak of measles in the Oregon Territory. The disease spread to the Cayuse Indians around the mission of Dr. Marcus Whitman, near the present Walla Walla, Washington. Dr. Whitman, a physician, had come west in 1836 with his beautiful blonde bride, Narcissa, one of the first two white women

127

The assassination of Marcus Whitman, as an artist imagined it.

to cross the Rockies. Although the physician worked untiringly to save the sick, he could not prevent deaths among the Indians. The disease was new to them; they had no immunity from exposures during childhood. A rumor spread quickly: the missionary had opened a measles bottle. Long resentful of the settlers who were taking their lands, the Indians killed the Whitmans and a dozen others.

The Oregon whites promptly declared war on the natives, who had no guns. The Indians were defeated and a few years later were confined to a reservation.

Many of the Oregonians who migrated to the gold country had fought in the Cayuse War. They were bitter against all Indians and sometimes expressed their hostility with gunfire. The Digger Indians of California quickly learned that the tall young mountaineers in buckskins were their enemies. If they saw a chance to eliminate one of these intruders, they struck.

The hostility between the Oregonians and the Diggers was deepened by another conflict. When gold was discovered, the established Californians hired Indians to dig and wash the metal. The Indians were paid according to the weight of the gold they found. The standard wage was a cheap calico shirt, worth $2 or $3, for gold dust worth $48. The Indians worked hard and their employers got richer every day.

The Oregonians needed Indian help, so they offered a better wage. They agreed to pay one shirt for only $32 worth of gold. This deal made the Californians angry because the Indians soon went over to the Oregon diggings where they could get more shirts. In retaliation, the Californians offered a shirt for $16 worth of gold. The Oregonians defied them by promising a shirt for only $8 in gold dust.

The shirt war soon became deadly. Oregon gold-seekers were murdered. The Californians insisted that the Indians were guilty, and there is no doubt that the Diggers had done some killing. But it seems just as certain that the Californians were encouraging the Indians to get rid of their competitors.

The gold country was ready for a bloody outbreak. It began when a war party of a dozen whites rode out from Old Greenwood's cabin to avenge the murder of two Oregon men. John Greenwood, the pathfinder's tall and handsome son, was one of the leaders.

"Be sure, boys, you bring me a squaw!" Old Greenwood shouted as the horsemen left for an Indian *rancheria*.

"Bring *me* a scalp!" the New Yorker, Osgood, called as a joke.

The next morning Caleb was storming around his cabin, cursing loudly enough to shake the pines.

"They say the Injuns have killed my son, but it's a lie, a damned infernal lie, they can't kill John Greenwood, he's

129

Mining at Murderer's Bar on the Middle Fork, American River.

a brave boy, they can't kill him, I say. I've lived among Injuns all my life, I know the varmints, and they know me —shot over a hundred of 'em in my time—shot ten in this valley, and ain't done with the bloody villains yet."

The Indians didn't kill John Greenwood or anyone else in the party that had raided the *rancheria*. But four Indians had died, and the village had been burnt. Young Greenwood, who soon returned, had killed three men, shooting one through the heart at a distance of 150 yards. As he rode past Osgood, he flung a bloody scalp to the ground. Disgusted, Osgood threw it into the millrace.

This raid was small, compared with one organized soon after by the Oregonians in reprisal for the killing of five men on the Middle Fork of the American River. The raiders killed 27 Indians in their *rancheria* and brought 40 prison-

130

The South Fork of the American River now covers Sutter's Mill site.

ers back to Coloma for a trial. Two of the prisoners were declared guilty, five others were suspected of guilt, and the rest were released. The seven held as prisoners were taken to a triangular space bounded by the hills, the village and the swollen river. Sure of their doom, they suddenly broke and ran. The whites opened fire. Two Indians dropped instantly; three got to the hills but two were overtaken and stabbed to death. Two jumped into the icy water and were shot or stoned. Only one escaped.

The massacre angered Old Greenwood. One witness said he tossed his arms aloft with violent denunciation, then stooped down to gather dust which he sprinkled on his head, swearing that he was innocent of the Indians' blood. John Greenwood, who had been a member of the raiding party, stood by in silence. He had not joined in the killings.

131

James W. Marshall in 1884, when he was 74.

There were other whites who were outraged by the mob's action. One of them was James Marshall, who was forced by the hotheads to leave Coloma for a time. Captain Sutter was another fair-minded pioneer. When he was asked to intervene in the war he declined, saying he might be able to reason with the Indians but his life would be endangered by the mob.

17
His Rifle by His Side

THE LAST WRITTEN RECORD of Caleb Greenwood is found in an 1849 account book of Shannon and Cady, proprietors of a general store in Coloma. Seven items were charged to him under the name of "Old Greenwood." On April 18 he bought a bottle of whisky for $6 and a candle for $1. The next day he ordered "liquor" for $1, a pint of vinegar at $1, another bottle of whisky for $6 and a bottle of ale for $5. The final purchase was a bottle of ale on April 20. At that point the storekeepers may have decided that Old Greenwood's alcohol capacity exceeded his financial ability and cut off his credit. There is no record of further purchases and there is no indication that the bill was ever paid.

In the summer of 1849, Old Greenwood left the cabin in Coloma and moved his family about ten miles north to Greenwood Valley, site of the present town of Greenwood. This was where Caleb invited Henry DeGroot to settle their differences with a rifle after the futile search for Gold Lake.

Several reasons may have prompted the move. Certainly the miners of Coloma did not feel kindly toward Caleb and John after the Gold Lake hoax. It is probable that young Angeline Greenwood died at Coloma, and her father may have sought a healthier climate for her sisters and brothers. Another factor may have been an opportunity to make money by selling to the miners, who were spreading all over

133

the country. John Greenwood was able to set up a trading post in Greenwood Valley with $1,046 worth of supplies obtained on credit from Shannon and Cady on May 7. The stock included such essentials as pickles and lead, brandy and rice. Most of the bill was soon paid, but a balance of $338 was owed at the end of the month. On August 10 John made a visit to Coloma that apparently conformed to the traditions of a gold rush town. He went to Shannon and Cady's store, but he did not settle his debt. The final Greenwood entry in the account book was: "Jno. Greenwood: 1 bottle champagne, $8; 3 broken glasses, $3." Shannon and Cady had lost again.

Tents were pitched in Greenwood Valley as the miners

Annie L. Spencer

The white arrow marks Old Greenwood's whisky purchase. Directly beneath, "50 lbs. Flour" were probably bought by James Marshall.

The town of Greenwood in 1967. Kemp's Grocery is no longer open.

worked claims along Greenwood Creek above and below its junction with Jackass Creek. The settlement soon became known as Greenwood, and it prospered. Historical Landmark 521 of the California State Park Commission says that Greenwood once had a theater, 4 hotels, 14 stores, a brewery and 4 saloons. After the gold rush the town began to shrink. The last hotel was torn down in the 1930s and by 1967 there were only two taverns, a gas station and a tiny post office. Oddly, the historical monument mentions only John Greenwood, "a trapper and guide who came to

135

California in 1844," as the founder of the community. Old Caleb is ignored on the bronze plate.

The Greenwoods did not stay long in the beautiful little valley between the South and Middle Forks of the American River. Apparently they moved 30 miles north to the South Fork of the Yuba River, near present Nevada City, for there are several reports of "Greenwood's Camp" there in 1849. Perhaps this camp was used by John when he was hunting for Gold Lake. One miner wrote, however, that he had prospected in a claim "that had just been abandoned by the notorious Greenwood," and this meant Caleb.

Sometime between the fall of 1849 and the spring of 1850, Caleb died, probably at the age of 87. No one yet knows when or where he died, or where he was buried. There are three clues to his death. A Forty-niner from Ohio, John Edward Banks, wrote in his diary for March 24, 1850, that he was encamped in Greenwood Valley where Greenwood "was recently found dead under a tree; liquor was his executioner." Next, Colonel John E. Ross, a gold-hunter from Oregon, recalled in 1878 that Caleb died "in 1849 between Bear River and Yuba River." Finally, Mrs. Sarah E. Healy wrote at about the same time that Old Greenwood had died in the mining country, somewhere near Oroville.

"I heard a report that he insisted on lying out of doors, with his rifle by his side, and would not allow even a tent over his body to obscure the sky—threatening to shoot the man who should attempt to put a shelter over him."

Mrs. Healy's recollection of the scene of Caleb's death —"somewhere near Oroville"—is close to Ross's location of "between Bear River and Yuba River." This would be about 30 miles southeast of Oroville, in the vicinity of Greenwood's Camp at Nevada City. And so it may have been that Old Greenwood's trail ended close by the route of the emigrants crossing the Sierra, close by the route he had often traveled—the last time to rescue the Donner party.

136

The death of the great mountain man created one final legend, a legend that Charles Kelly believes is close to the truth. The story is that in his last days Caleb had no one with him except his son James, a boy of about nine. Feeble and sometimes confused, the old man dreamed he was sleeping under the bright stars of the mountains, only to awake and find himself staring at the dark timbers of the cabin roof.

"Where in tarnation am I?" he demanded.

"You're at home, dad, home in your own cabin. Don't you remember?"

"Cabin be damned!" the old mountaineer shouted. "When did Old Greenwood git so infernally soft he has to sleep in a confounded cabin like a white-livered emigrator? 'Taint no place to sleep—can't git my breath. Got to git out where I can see the sky, son. It's too damned dark in here."

Grabbing his gun and worn buffalo robe, Caleb tottered from the cabin. He found a piece of level ground with no stones or roots and made his bed as he used to, under the sky.

"You'll catch your death o' dampness out here," James argued. His father paid no attention.

Later in the evening, when a damp chill spread through the valley, James decided to raise a small tent over his sleeping father. No sooner had the boy approached with canvas and poles than Caleb awoke with a growl.

"Git away from me and let me alone," he shouted, "before I fill yer lousy carcass full o' hot lead. I'm a-goin' to sleep out here under the sky where I can git a breath o' air, like a man should, an' the first sneakin' varmint that tries to put an infernal tent over me is a dead Injun."

Knowing that his father meant what he said, James went back to the cabin and lay down on his bunk. When the first light of morning filtered through the pine tops, Old Greenwood was dead.

The lonely boy did not know what to do. He could not

Above: When Postmistress Viola Anderson isn't in, you press a buzzer.

Below: Greenwood Creek, a mere trickle, once rang with miners' picks.

dig a grave by himself. He dared not leave, lest the body be torn apart by wild animals and vultures. For three days he waited, hoping that gold-seekers or a pack train might pass within hailing distance. None came, so James finally went to find help. He was lucky enough to meet a party of miners just a few miles from camp, and they returned with him to the cabin.

A grave was soon dug, but there was not a scrap of lumber for a coffin. One of the miners had an idea. He picked out a large pine, which was felled. The heavy bark was split from the trunk in two sections like the two halves of a pea pod. Old Greenwood, wrapped in his buffalo robe, was laid in one section and covered with the other. The bark coffin was lowered into the grave. The miners went back to work with their shovels, and in a few minutes the burial was finished.

Today there is no trace of Greenwood's Camp, and no one knows where that last cabin stood. Although the pathfinder's name has remained on the land with the names of a post office, creek and valley in El Dorado County, and of a creek, ridge and town in Mendocino County, the spot where he probably died is nameless.

Perhaps a sketch of Caleb himself may be found some day among the papers of a Forty-niner who was also an artist. Yet if none ever turns up, one picture will be clear in the reader's mind: A towering figure in white hair, white beard, and worn buckskin, blazing new trails in the west, and finally lying down with his rifle by his side.

ALEXANDER L. CROSBY was born in Maryland and grew up in California, where he was graduated from the University of California. He returned to the east for newspaper work, and in the WPA period he edited the *New Jersey Guide* of the American Guide Series. Since 1944 he has been a free-lance writer.

In August 1967 Mr. Crosby drove through much of the country that Old Greenwood traveled, making photographs for this book. He was accompanied and often guided by his wife, Nancy Larrick, author of *A Parent's Guide to Children's Reading* and other books.

The Crosbys live on 33 acres of fields and woods at Quakertown, Pennsylvania, where they feed a good many animals, from muskrats to Canada geese. Other books by Mr. Crosby are:

STEAMBOAT UP THE COLORADO

THE RIO GRANDE, LIFE FOR THE DESERT

THE COLORADO, MOVER OF MOUNTAINS

THE RIMAC, RIVER OF PERU

THE JUNIOR SCIENCE BOOK OF BEAVERS

THE JUNIOR SCIENCE BOOK OF POND LIFE

THE JUNIOR SCIENCE BOOK OF CANADA
    GEESE

THE WORLD OF ROCKETS

INDEX

144